ABIDE IN ME

Abide in Me

*A Daily Guide
to Prayer and Meditation*

David E. Rosage

Abide in Me

Copyright © 1985 by David E. Rosage
All rights reserved
Hardcover edition published in 1987

Book design by John B. Leidy.
Front cover photograph from H. Armstrong Roberts.

Published by Servant Books
P.O. Box 8617
Ann Arbor, Michigan 48107

This edition reprinted in 1992 by SMITHMARK Publishers
Inc., 16 East 32nd Street, New York, NY 10016; (212) 532-6600.

SMITHMARK books are available for bulk purchase for sales
promotion and premium use. For details write or call the
manager of special sales, SMITHMARK Publishers Inc.,
16 East 32nd Street, New York, NY 10016; (212) 532-6600.

Library of Congress Cataloging-in-Publication Data
Rosage, David E.
    Abide in me: a daily guide to prayer and meditation/
David E. Rosage
        p.   cm.
    Originally published: Ann Arbor, Mich.:
Servant Books, c1985.
        ISBN: 0-8317-4976-8: $4.98
    1. Devotional calendars—Catholic Church.   2. Catholic
Church—Prayer-books and   devotions—English.   I. Title.
BX2182.2.R8473   1992
242'.2—dc20   92-19811
                                                        CIP

Printed in the United States of America

10 9 8 7 6 5 4 3 2

*To all our mothers, fathers, and
teachers who gently, patiently,
and lovingly led us along
pathways into prayer.*

Contents

Introduction

MANY TIMES WE HAVE HEARD the lament: "I wish I had enough leisure time to spend some moments in prayer each day." *Abide in Me* is a compilation of themes taken from scripture that form an ideal basis for our daily visit with the Lord.

Abide in Me is being offered as a guideline, or handbook, for people who have little time for prayer and also for those who feel that they are too busy to pray. *Follow Me*, a previous book, has helped so many in their personal relationship with God that many readers have requested a sequel. *Abide in Me* is a continuation of *Follow Me*.

Format

The twelve chapters correspond to the twelve months of the year. Each month has a specific theme. A brief scriptural passage is suggested for each day of the month. This passage augments the overall theme of the month. The scriptural text is followed by a brief commentary. This short commentary is of secondary importance, but it is intended to stimulate some thoughts for reflection on the words of scripture. The scripture passage should be read and re-read reflectively until the word finds a home in our hearts.

Dwelling on the same topic throughout the month will help our hearts form a habit-pattern which governs our attitudes and actions. Repeating the same theme with different scriptural passages will aid us in forming a dynamic Christian habit-pattern which will greatly influence our daily life. We may not even notice the transformation taking place within us.

The scripture passages offered here are very brief and may not be fully understood if taken out of context. For a richer, deeper understanding, it is best to read the whole passage in the Bible to better comprehend the message which the Lord is trying to convey.

The closing days of the month usually center on an episode taken from the gospels that capsulizes the theme of the previous weeks.

How to Use This Book

The selections in this volume are intended to help us experience a greater awareness of the Lord's abiding love and presence with us throughout each day. This deeper awareness will bring us peace and joy. Using the following method should prove fruitful:

1. Before retiring at night, read slowly and reflectively the scriptural passage for the next day. If time and energy permit, read the whole section in the Bible as well as the short commentary.

2. In the morning reread the passage and use it as a springboard for prayer. Throughout the day pause for a few seconds to recall the message the Lord spoke to you during your time of prayer. This procedure will make you more consciously aware of the presence of the Lord with you at all times. "And know that I am with you always, until the end of the world!" (Mt 28:20).

3. Keep a journal; it is a marvelous tool for greater growth and real maturity in your life of prayer. Journal-keeping is also an ideal way to obtain spiritual direction. The repetition of daily journal writing is invaluable in forming habit-patterns of living in the Lord's presence.

Family or Group Prayer

Married couples, families, or groups can easily follow this same procedure. Begin in the evening by reading the scripture together. Afterward, share some thoughts about the passage. During the course of the day each family member should pause and recall the presence of the Lord and the message he imparted to them in his word. Doing so will enrich the sharing that evening at the dinner table. This kind of praying and sharing will enhance the love relationship between husband and wife and will knit the whole family in bonds of love. It will make your journey through life more joyous and peaceful.

With the Father's grace and blessing, may each day spent with his word bring us closer to the Author and Giver of life and love.

FIRST MONTH

Trinitarian Love

T HE THOUGHT THAT GOD loves us personally and individually is overwhelming.
We cannot comprehend such a great
mystery. In sacred scripture God tells us
that he loves us just as we are, regardless of
who we are or what we might have done.
We are loved by all three Persons of the
Blessed Trinity. The Father loves us with a
creative love; Jesus loves us with a redeeming love; the Holy Spirit loves us with
a sanctifying love.

Through the prophets of the Old Testament the Father reveals how much he
loves us. His love for us is faithful and
forgiving, enduring and eternal.

Jesus' entire life on earth was one continuous manifestation of his love for us. He
proclaimed the good news and showed us
the way to salvation so that we might be
with him for all eternity. He freely laid
down his life to redeem us. Even more, he
rose from the dead to share his risen life
with us.

The Holy Spirit proves his boundless

love for us as he carries on the work of sanctification within us. He loves us so much that he abides with us making temples of our bodies. By his divine presence and power, the Holy Spirit purifies, sanctifies, energizes, and strengthens us because he loves us.

During this month, as we ponder a scripture passage for each day and let it find a home in our heart, we will experience and appreciate God's love for us more fully. We will find much joy in responding to his love.

1 *"You are precious in my eyes / and glorious and . . . I love you."* (Is 43:4)

Let God love you! We are so busy trying to do something for God that it is difficult for us to take time to rest in his presence and let him love us. Pause right now and relax in the sunshine of his presence and love. Listen to him calling you by name and saying: "You are precious to me. I love you."

Let that refrain repeat itself in your heart so that you can form the habit-pattern of knowing at the core of your being that you are loved and lovable.

2 *"I will never forget you. / See, upon the palm of my hands I have written your name."*
(Is 49:15-16)

To hold someone in the palms of our hands is a semitic expression meaning that we will never forget them. Our Father in heaven promises that he will never forget us because his love is infinite and immutable. He loves us with a love that is unconditional and eternal. This knowledge brings peace and joy and a yearning to respond to such gracious love.

3 *"For I know well the plans I have in mind for you, says the Lord, plans for your welfare, not for woe!"* (Jer 29:11)

We may be anxious, worried, or per-plexed by certain happenings in our daily life, especially when trials and sufferings, heartaches and disappointments come our way. In God's providential plan all these difficulties serve a specific purpose. They are for our welfare. From a future point of view, we may look back to discover that something which seemed at one time to be tragic was really a wondrous blessing. God's plans are always for our welfare, even though disguised at times.

4 *"With an age-old love I have loved you; / so I have kept my mercy toward you."* (Jer 31:3)

God's word is eternal. He loves us from the beginning of time, and his love will continue for all eternity without change or alteration.

When we love a person, we want to give that person something they want or to perform a service that they need. Mercy is an expression of love. Since God loves us, he is eager and anxious to manifest his mercy by forgiving and healing us when-ever we turn to him with contrite hearts.

5 *"With great tenderness I will take you back....
/ With enduring love I take pity on you, / says
the Lord, your redeemer."* (Is 54:7-8)

Sin is a rejection of God's love. Sin is
saying no to love, but that does not alter
God's love for us. He assures us that his
love is an "enduring love." God knows our
human weakness. He understands how
prone we are to evil. He waits for us! The
Lord of heaven and earth waits for us
to turn back to him. He waits for us to
acknowledge our sinfulness; then he says,
"With great tenderness I will take you
back."

6 *"My love shall never leave you / nor my
covenant of peace be shaken, / says the Lord,
who has mercy on you."* (Is 54:10)

Conscious of our own sinfulness, we
may feel unworthy to be loved and accepted by God, our Father. Ingrained
within us is the notion that we must earn or
deserve God's love. But God's love is
immutable; it never changes. We are the
ones who change, either by opening wide
to the Father's love or by restricting his
love from flowing into us. When doubts,
misgivings, or fear of not being lovable
assails us, we need to pause and listen with
all our heart to the Father saying: "My love
shall never leave you."

7 *Yes, God so loved the world / that he gave his only Son, / that whoever believes in him may not die / but may have eternal life.* (Jn 3:16)

By sin the human race severed its relationship with God. We were helpless, lost; salvation was impossible. But love always reaches out to a need. And God responded to our need by giving us the greatest gift possible—the gift of himself in the Person of Jesus.

We can appreciate this gift even more when we consider the price of our redemption—death on a cross. Yet how easy the Father made our salvation. Whoever believes in Jesus and lives accordingly will have eternal life.

8 *"As the Father has loved me, / so I have loved you. / Live on in my love."* (Jn 15:9)

The Father loves Jesus with an infinite love. This is perfect love. Jesus assures us that he loves us with that same degree of love.

God created us with a desire to be accepted, to be loved. This reassurance that Jesus gives us is the source of genuine happiness for us. Jesus bids us to live on in his love, enjoying the peace, joy, and happiness which it brings us even in this life. This is already a bit of heaven.

9 *"The Father already loves you, / because you have loved me / and have believed that I came from God."* (Jn 16:27)

Love generates faith. The more we love a person, the greater will be our faith, our confidence, and our trust in that person. When we believe all that Jesus revealed and when we are striving to live his way of life and put on his mind and heart, then we know that the Father loves us.

There is no greater joy than knowing that we are loved by God. His love assures us that we are loved and lovable.

10 *"There is no greater love than this: / to lay down one's life for one's friends."*

(Jn 15:13)

This pronouncement of Jesus overwhelms us. Even more startling is the fact that the very next day he did lay down his life for us. As the Good Shepherd, he promised that he would give up his life for us and that no one would take it away from him, but that he would lay it down freely. Paul reminds us: "It is precisely in this that God proves his love for us; that while we were still sinners, Christ died for us" (Rom 5:8).

11 *"He who obeys the commandments he has from me / is the one who loves me; / and he who loves me will be loved by my Father. / I too will love him / and reveal myself to him."*

(Jn 14:21)

Love always wants to please. Jesus fulfilled his Father's will perfectly, not out of slavish obedience, but to please his Father. Every act of obedience was a love-offering. Jesus reminded us many times in the gospel that he had come to do the Father's will.

We manifest our love for Jesus by obeying his commandments. The reward is great. Jesus will love us and continue to reveal more and more of himself to us.

12 *"Such as my love has been for you, / so must your love be for each other."* (Jn 13:34)

Jesus really threw us a curve ball when he told us how much we are to love our neighbor: "Such as my love has been for you." That ideal may seem virtually impossible until we realize that Jesus is pouring his love into us so that it may overflow to others. We are to be channels whereby his love can touch others. With Jesus' love operating within us, loving others is easier.

13 *"This is my commandment: / love one another / as I have loved you."* (Jn 15:12)

Most people who find it difficult to love another person are usually insecure people with low self-images. However, when we know that Jesus loves us just as we are and that his love will never change, it becomes much easier to reach out in love to others. Knowing that we are loved and lovable enables us to love others without being threatened. Then this commandment of Jesus seems more attainable.

14 *"That all may be one / as you, Father, are in me, and I in you; / I pray that they may be one in us, / that the world may believe that you sent me."* (Jn 17:21)

Love includes the desire to share life with a loved one. Love wants to be united with the beloved. This longing is inherent in genuine love. In his prayer, Jesus prayed that we may be united with him and the Father in a union of perfect love. We have been baptized into the trinitarian life which is a community of perfect love. We are destined for that kind of perfect love. The more we strive for it in this life, the more certain we are of obtaining it in the life hereafter.

15 *"Father, / all those you gave me / I would have in my company / where I am, / to see this glory of mine."* (Jn 17:24)

Jesus loves us so much that he wants us to be with him at all times. Jesus wants us to attain our heavenly home more than we could even want it ourselves. He asks the Father that we might be with him in his glory for all eternity. There is much comfort and reassurance in this prayer of Jesus. With our eyes set on this goal, there is no cross too burdensome for us to bear during our earthly pilgrimage.

16 *Of his fullness / we have all had a share— / love following upon love. . . . / This enduring love came through Jesus Christ.*

(Jn 1:16-17)

Jesus' love for us is certainly an enduring love. His sojourn on earth was one continuous manifestation of his love. He proclaimed the good news of salvation. He comforted and consoled. He forgave and healed. His love reached a climax after the resurrection when he shared his glorified life with us. His enduring love continues as he carries on his redemptive work which is his glory at the right hand of the Father.

17 *"I will ask the Father / and he will give you another Paraclete— / to be with you always: / the Spirit of truth, / whom the world cannot accept, / since it neither sees him nor recognizes him; / but you can recognize him / because he remains with you / and will be within you."* (Jn 14:16-17)

This solemn promise of Jesus, made at the last supper, was fulfilled on Pentecost when the Holy Spirit poured his divine life upon the apostles. That same promise is fulfilled in each one of us at the moment of our baptism. Jesus was pleased to promise us the Holy Spirit. The Father was delighted to send us the Spirit, and the Spirit rejoices to remain with us and be within us.

18 *The love of God has been poured out in our hearts through the Holy Spirit who has been given to us.* (Rom 5:5)

The Holy Spirit is the Niagara Falls of divine love being poured into us. He is the very source of love. His work of sanctification is wrought through his love. His love brings with it his special gifts of wisdom, knowledge, and understanding, enabling us to seek out and follow the path to happiness in this life and guaranteeing us a life of eternal bliss with the Trinity.

19 *You must know that your body is a temple of the Holy Spirit, who is within—the Spirit you have received from God. You are not your own. You have been purchased, and at a price! So glorify God in your body.* (1 Cor 6:19)

When Jesus redeemed our human nature, he endowed us with the capacity to receive his divine life and love. At baptism we are made the temples of the Holy Spirit, who continues to live with us and within us filling us with his divine life and love. This sharing in the life of God binds us all together as the family of God. We are brothers and sisters to each other because we have a common source of life, the Holy Spirit.

20 *The fruit of the spirit is love, joy, peace, patient endurance, kindness, generosity, faith, mildness and chastity.* (Gal 5:22-23)

The principal fruit of the Holy Spirit is love. All the other fruits of the Spirit are component parts of love. Peace, joy, patience, and all the other fruits flow from love as from an inexhaustible fountain. As we become more and more receptive to the influx of the Spirit's love, we will radiate the peace, joy, kindness, patience, generosity, and faith which he generates within us.

21 *So may God, the source of hope, fill you with all joy and peace in believing so that through the power of the Holy Spirit you may have hope in abundance.* (Rom 15:13)

Our pathway through life is often strewn with difficulties, worries, anxieties, and problems. We need hope at every crossroad in life. When we have "hope in abundance," we can keep our heads raised high, a smile on our lips, and our vision clear. We can journey along with "all the joy and peace" which the Holy Spirit showers so abundantly upon us. Because the Holy Spirit loves us so much, he continues to fill us with hope every step of the way.

22 *The Spirit God has given us is no cowardly spirit, but rather one that makes us strong, loving, and wise.* (2 Tm 1:7)

The way of life to which Jesus is calling us may seem difficult to live at times. Certainly it is unpopular in our secular world. Jesus was well aware that we might become discouraged and even tempted to abandon his way. This is why he promised and sent us the Holy Spirit. The Holy Spirit is the powerhouse energizing us to dare to be different. He gives us the wisdom to recognize the way of life to which we are called. He is the source of strength and courage needed to follow that way.

23 *If the Spirit of him who raised Jesus from the dead dwells in you, then he who raised Christ from the dead will bring your mortal bodies to life also, through his Spirit dwelling in you.* (Rom 8:11)

The Holy Spirit dwells with us to enlighten, encourage, and strengthen us by filling us with his love. Because he comes to dwell in us as his temples, we already have one foot in heaven. We enjoy as much of his divine life as our mortal bodies are capable of receiving.

Death is our transition into God's divine life in all its fullness. The Spirit brings us to Jesus who, in turn, presents us to the Father. We will then live in that community of perfect love for all eternity.

24 *The Spirit too helps us in our weakness, for we do not know how to pray as we ought; but the Spirit himself makes intercession for us with groanings that cannot be expressed in speech.* (Rom 8:26)

Prayer establishes our relationship with God. Prayer is our loving response to the outpouring of God's love upon us. This is a gift of the Holy Spirit. The Holy Spirit envelops our spirit, enabling us to penetrate our human ego and bask in the presence of God. This type of prayer has enormous transforming power.

"Anyone Who Loves Me"

Anyone who loves me / will be true to my word, / and my Father will love him; / we will come to him / and make our dwelling place with him. / He who does not love me does not keep my words. / Yet the word you hear is not mine; / it comes from the Father who sent me. / This much have I told you while I was still with you; / the Paraclete, the Holy Spirit / whom the Father will send in my name, / will instruct you in everything, / and remind you of all that I told you. (Jn 14:23-26)

25 *"Anyone who loves me / will be true to my word." (Jn 14:23)*

Jesus' word to us is a reminder that we are blessed with a unique love—the love of the Holy Trinity: Father, Son, and Holy Spirit. The Father loves us with a creating love and continues to recreate us at every moment of the day. Jesus' redemptive love is operative within us, forgiving, healing, and redeeming us all day long. The Holy Spirit is pouring his sanctifying love into us, enlightening, guiding, and strengthening us on our path through life. Responding to the word of Jesus is our way of loving in return.

26 *"My Father will love him."* (Jn 14:23)

The Father loves Jesus with an infinite love (Jn 15:9). Jesus tells us that he loves us with that same infinite love. Since the Father and Jesus are one, then, the Father loves us with an infinite love.

We know the Father loves us because the message that Jesus brought is the good news which the Father asked Jesus to announce to us. Our response to that message greatly pleases the Father.

27 *"We will come to him / and make our dwelling place with him."* (Jn 14:23)

Dwelling place has a twofold connotation. First, if we lovingly observe and obey Jesus' word, we will be assured of our eternal happiness in heaven in union with the Holy Trinity.

Second, the Trinity will make a dwelling place with us here and now, in this life. We already have a foretaste of heaven even in this life. We "are the temples of the Living God" (2 Cor 6:16). In baptism we were adopted as sons and daughters of our Father. We are members of the Body of Christ. We are already in the vestibule of heaven.

28 *"He who does not love me does not keep my words."* (Jn 14:24)

Jesus' words to us reveal the lifestyle he invites us to live. Living his words will bring us into a deeper, richer relationship with him. Only in this close union will we be able to know Jesus as a Person with our hearts.

We cannot love someone we do not know. Listening to his word will help us come to a fuller heart knowledge of him. Jesus will continue to reveal himself to us in the silent, listening moments of our prayer.

29 *"Yet the word you hear is not mine; / it comes from the Father who sent me."*
(Jn 14:24)

God respects our free will. He is a courteous God and will never force himself upon us. Revelation is not so much a matter of making truths and doctrines known, as it is God making himself known as a personal, loving Father.

The Father's word is a fuller, deeper revelation of himself. If we are humble and receptive, he will reveal himself more clearly to us and also give us greater insights into his fathomless love for us. If we are attuned to him at every moment of the day, we will discover insights otherwise hidden.

30 *"The Paraclete, the Holy Spirit / whom the Father will send in my name / will instruct you in everything."* (Jn 14:26)

After the glorification of Jesus, the Holy Spirit completes the revelation of Christ by enlightening the church concerning the true meaning of what Jesus did and taught. Only after the coming of the Holy Spirit on Pentecost did the apostles understand fully the mission of Jesus.

Today the Holy Spirit continues to clarify our mission in life and lead us by his divine love. He will be the source of our inspiration, motivation, and perseverance.

31 *"The paraclete, the Holy Spirit / . . . [will] remind you of all that I told you."*
(Jn 14:26)

In moments of discouragement and fear, the Holy Spirit will bring us hope and endurance. He will encourage and guide us in moments of hesitation and doubt, reminding us that God's providential plan for us is often wrapped in mystery. The Spirit will endow us with his special gifts of wisdom, knowledge, and understanding as we journey down life's highway. All of this he does because he loves us. This is the special work of the Holy Spirit as he fulfills his mission of sanctification.

Fear Is Useless

L OVE BEGETS TRUST. As we grow in love, the greater will be our trust. Our trust is proportionate to the credibility of the person in whom we place our trust. Can there be any person more credible than the Lord himself?

Strange as it may seem, we often trust other people more than our loving Father in heaven or Jesus himself. A partial reason may be that we know that another person is well aware of our human limitations and will not expect too much from us. On the other hand, we do not know how much God will ask of us. He may ask more than we are willing to give.

In his teaching Jesus repeatedly stressed the necessity of total trust and confidence in him and in his Father. Our trust must be the same as that of a little child who places implicit trust in his father's loving care and concern.

If our confidence in God is childlike, then we will be convinced that whatever happens in life is either according to God's direct will or his permissive will and that it is for our welfare. Such a disposition of mind and heart requires total trust in God.

As we reflect on the gospel we will discover how pleased Jesus is when he finds faith and trust in him. On the other hand, he decries a lack of trust in him.

Our reflection this month focuses on trust as exemplified in God's word. As our confidence and trust increases, our love will also mature. This is the source of great peace and joy.

1 *"Father, Lord of heaven and earth, to you I offer praise; for what you have hidden from the learned and the clever you have revealed to the merest children."* (Mt 11:25)

Jesus was thrilled that ordinary people were able to comprehend his teachings. He regretted that the leaders were unwilling to listen with an open mind and heart. Jesus was so pleased that he paused in his teaching to pray on location: "Father, I offer you praise."

It requires humility and trust to come to the Lord with a listening, trusting heart, rather than to accept only what our limited minds can comprehend. This is childlike faith. This is childlike trust. This is childlike humility.

2 *"Whoever makes himself lowly, becoming like this child, is of greatest importance in that heavenly reign."* (Mt 18:4)

A child sets many patterns for our Christian behavior. A child is humble. A child is instinctively dependent and instinctively trusts others, especially parents. A child has the power of wonder, of awe and reverence, which leads him to the divine. A child has the power to forgive and forget. All these qualities are the attitudes and dispositions with which Jesus challenges his followers.

3 *"I assure you, unless you change and become like little children, you will not enter the kingdom of God."* (Mt 18:3)

Jesus calls for a change of heart, a conversion, a metanoia in our lives. He knows that our spirit of pride, of self-sufficiency and independence often prevents his gifts and graces from operating within us. Jesus holds up the attitude of a little child as an ideal frame of mind and disposition of heart enabling his divine life to mold and transform us.

Pray for that childlike trust!

4 *"Whoever welcomes this little child on my account welcomes me, and whoever welcomes me welcomes him who sent me; for the least one among you is the greatest."* (Lk 9:48)

Jesus did not mean these words literally. Jesus wants us to have a childlike faith and trust in the way of life he taught. If we accept and believe his word, then we are also accepting the Father from whom the word originates. Confidently and trustingly believing and living his word will make us truly great in God's eyes.

5 *O Lord, my heart is not proud, / nor are my eyes haughty; / I busy not myself with great things, / nor with things too sublime for me.*
(Ps 131:1)

In this prayer we are reminded of the need to keep our focus on the proper end in life. If we are striving to reach goals for which we are not equipped or are motivated by inordinate desires for things which cannot satisfy us but rather lead us away from God, then we are destined for a life of misery, frustration, and unhappiness.

On the other hand, accepting ourselves for what we are, enjoying the gifts and talents the Lord has given us will bring great peace, joy, and happiness.

6 *I have stilled and quieted / my soul like a weaned child. / Like a weaned child on its mother's lap.* (Ps 131:2)

A weaned child is content to rest quietly on its mother's lap. The child is not seeking food, only love. Stillness permits the mother to love her child. The child's presence resting on its mother's lap is also a way of expressing its love for the mother.

Our resting in stillness and silence in the sunshine of the Lord's presence is a means of expressing our love. In turn the Lord is saturating us with his love.

7 *As an eagle incites its nestlings forth / by hovering over its brood, / So he spread his wings to receive them / and bore them up on his pinions.* (Dt 32:11)

When an eagle builds its nest, it puts rough objects in the bottom, then covers them with soft down. When its young are ready to fly, the mother tosses out the softness to force the young birds to saunter forth and try their wings. This is a traumatic experience. When a young bird shows signs of weakness in flying, the mother swoops down under it and rescues it on her pinions.

This graphically describes what our loving Father does for us. He first conditions us for our mission in life. Then, as we launch out, he stands by ready to come to our rescue if we have the trust of a child.

8 *"Trust God and he will help you; / make straight your ways and hope in him."*
(Sir 2:6)

Trust is part of love. We cannot love the Lord unless we know him as a personal God. We cannot know him unless we take time to prayerfully listen to him at the very core of our being. This kind of prayer helps us "make straight our ways" and augments our "hope in him." As our love increases, so does our trust in him.

9 *"Do not fear, Mary. You have found favor with God."* (Lk 1:30)

The angel's message could have been disturbing to Mary; hence, at the outset, the angel gave her the reassurance: "You have found favor with God."

When we experience God's presence or power in us or around us, we stand in awe and reverence. Our hearts may become fearful. There might be a frightening expectancy of what might happen. Mary's faith and trust should help allay our fears.

10 *"Blest is she who trusted that the Lord's words to her would be fulfilled."* (Lk 1:45)

Mary our mother was a person of great faith. She was asked to fulfill a role which had never been heard of in the annals of human history. When she was asked to become the mother of God, she accepted without hesitation. She was the temple of the Holy Spirit, and she permitted him to work freely in her life. She uttered her *fiat* because she realized "nothing is impossible with God" (Lk 1:37).

11 *"I give you my word, if you are ready to believe that you will receive whatever you ask for in prayer, it shall be done for you."*
(Mk 11:24)

A deep, abiding faith is the fruit of love, confidence, and trust. When we pray with expectant faith, Jesus promised that we would never be disappointed. On the other hand, if our faith is not a vibrant faith, our prayer, too, will be only half-hearted.

Imagine the joy in the heart of Jesus as he responds to a prayer vibrant with trust and confidence.

12 *"I do believe! Help my lack of trust!"*
(Mk 9:24)

The father of the possessed boy truly wanted to believe that Jesus could help him; hence he pleaded for ever greater trust. In our need we often come to the Lord to ask his help. At times we may ask only faint-heartedly, wondering if the Lord will really hear our plea. In our humanness we may doubt or even fear that God will not grant what we need.

Jesus reminds us that if we really believe and trust in him, he will grant whatever is good for us.

13 *"Get hold of yourselves! It is I. Do not be afraid!"* (Mk 6:50)

This gospel account of the storm at sea is symbolic of the trials and temptations, the difficulties and misunderstandings which arise frequently in our own lives. When these tempests assail us, we usually seek counsel and comfort from others. When we cannot find a satisfactory solution, we eventually turn to the Lord.

Jesus is reminding us that he is always with us and that he understands our plight. He reminds us: "It is I. Do not be afraid."

14 *"Fear is useless. What is needed is trust."* (Mk 5:36)

Fear can become paralyzing. It can warp our thinking. It can make us irrational. Our heavenly Father wishes to allay our fears when he assures us that his plans for us are for our welfare, not for woe (Jer 29:11).

Jesus reminds us that he is always with us. He begs us to trust him. A dynamic, operative faith in him will conquer all fear. With the father of the stricken boy, let us often pray: "Help the little trust I have."

15 *"Everything is possible to a man who trusts."* (Mk 9:23)

At times we may not undertake a good work because of our fear of failure. Our low self-image may tantalize us into feeling incapable of accomplishing a certain task even though the Lord may be calling us to it. We need to remember that when Jesus said: "Apart from me you can do nothing," he was really saying, "with me you can do all things." He asks us to trust him.

16 *"Are you confident I can do this? ... Because of your faith it shall be done to you."*
(Mt 9:28-29)

Jesus gladly restored sight to the two blind men because of their urgent prayer and because they had confidence in his healing power. Our prayer of faith will lift the blindness from our eyes that we may see the will of God in our own lives and have the confidence and trust in him we need to follow it.

17 *Trust in the Lord with all your heart / on your own intelligence rely not; / In all your ways be mindful of him, / and he will make straight your paths.* (Prv 3:5-6)

Love begets confidence and trust. If we keep ourselves aware of the Lord's loving concern for us, then we will trust him. If we are faced with a perplexing problem, we will not rely on our own intelligence but trust him to show us the way, since he makes our paths straight.

In the quiet time of our prayer, we can almost hear him saying to us: "Trust me! Trust me!"

18 *Cast your care upon the Lord, / and he will support you; / never will he permit the just man to be disturbed.* (Ps 55:23)

In the Psalter we are encouraged more frequently and more convincingly than in any other book of the Bible to place our complete confidence and trust in the Lord.

When a friend betrays us, when we are rejected, falsely accused, criticized, or misunderstood, we can always find comfort in knowing that the Lord will never desert us. If we are able to cast all our cares upon the Lord, we will be able to keep our heads erect, a smile on our lips, and a song in our hearts.

19 *And he put a new song into my mouth, / a hymn to our God. / Many shall look on in awe / and trust in the Lord.* (Ps 40:4)

If we confidently place all our trust in the Lord, we will radiate peace and joy. Our trusting disposition, regardless of the hills and valleys in our own lives, will automatically reflect itself to others and draw them into an attitude of greater trust and confidence in the Lord. This is part of our mission in life.

20 *For in him our hearts rejoice; / in his holy name we trust.* (Ps 33:21)

We have good reason to rejoice, because Jesus promised: "All you ask the Father in my name he will give you" (Jn 15:16). Not only will the Father respond to our prayer, but Jesus himself will grant our need. "Anything you ask in my name I will do" (Jn 14:14). Such extravagant promises cause our hearts to rejoice as we place our complete trust in our loving Father.

21 *Let your kindness come to me, O Lord, / your salvation according to your promises. / So shall I have an answer for those who reproach me, / for I trust in your words.* (Ps 119:41-42)

The Hebrew word *hesed* is an expression embracing the sum total of God's goodness. It has been variously translated as kindness, faithfulness, and goodness. When I begin to comprehend the kindness of the Lord, there is no reason why I should ever mistrust him.

For "those who reproach me" I shall then have a ready answer, "for I trust in your words."

22 *At dawn let me hear of your kindness, / for in you I trust. / Show me the way in which I should walk, / for to you I lift up my soul.*
(Ps 143:8)

If we begin the day by trusting that the Lord will be at our side all through the day, we will be happy and cheerful. If we trust him implicitly, he will take us by the hand enlightening, inspiring, strengthening, encouraging us as he shows us the path to follow. This reassurance will keep our hearts merry.

23 *For you are my hope, O Lord; / my trust, O God, from my youth.* (Ps 71:5)

As we look back over our lives, we will discover how fully our loving Father has cared for us and provided for our every need, from our earliest days to the present moment. Such a recollection will make us grateful and help us face each day with greater confidence and trust.

The Lord himself assures us of his enduring love: "My love will never leave you" (Is 54:10).

24 *Trust in him at all times, O my people! / Pour out your hearts before him; / God is our refuge!* (Ps 62:9)

God wants us to trust that he, in his goodness, will supply all our needs, but he also wants us to pour out our hearts before him. Vocalizing our petition will make it clearer in our own minds. It will also increase our dependence upon the Lord.

The psalmist appeals to us as a "people" to trust the Lord. Praying as a family, as a community, pleases God immeasurably, since it manifests our trust and confidence as a "faith community.'

The Promise of Glory

"Do not let your hearts be troubled. / Have faith in God / and faith in me. / In my Father's house there are many dwelling places; / otherwise, how could I have told you / that I was going to prepare a place for you? / And then I shall come back to take you with me, / that where I am you also may be. / You know the way that leads where I go." (Jn 14:1-4)

25 *"Do not let your hearts be troubled."* (Jn 14:1)

At this critical hour in Jesus' life, when the hatred of his enemies increased in intensity and viciousness and his death was imminent, he reached out beyond himself in loving concern for others. Jesus was thinking of us.

Darkness and fear may grip our hearts at times. We may feel alone and abandoned. If we let him love us at these times, his love will drive out the darkness and fear and fill our hearts with joy. This is what Jesus is trying to say: "Do not let your hearts be troubled."

26 *"Have faith in God / and faith in me."*
(Jn 14:1)

When the darkness descends and seems to envelop us, there is only one recourse—TRUST—trust that somehow whatever is taking place is for our good, for our spiritual growth and maturation.

When we believe in the promise of Jesus, our faith is pleasing to him. Even in the darkest hour our faith will bring a glimmer of hope. With the psalmist we pray: "I believe that I shall see the bounty of the Lord / in the land of the living" (Ps 27:13).

27 *"In my Father's house there are many dwelling places."* (Jn 14:2)

The "Father's house" is the presence of God. When we are aware of the presence of the Lord and enjoying his divine life and love, then we are in his "house." The "Father's house" is our eternal destiny, but we are already living in the vestibule of that house since Jesus is sharing his risen life with us.

We will partake in the fullness of his life and love when we shed this mortal body in death.

28 *"I am indeed going to prepare a place for you."* (Jn 14:3)

Jesus assures us that his departure is only temporary. He submits to his passion and death in order to redeem our fallen human nature. He will rise to a new, exalted, glorified life which he will share with us. This is his promise of eternal life for us.

Knowing that Jesus is always faithful to his promises, we can face any hardship, trial, or cross, assured that each is a stepping stone into a deeper union with him.

29 *"I shall come back to take you with me."* (Jn 14:3)

Jesus will certainly come back in triumph at his Second Coming. However, his return is more immediate. He has come to live with us through the power of the Holy Spirit.

Jesus will also be with us at the time of our death to take us to the Father. Since we will not be alone, we have nothing to fear, realizing that the Father and Jesus want our eternal salvation even more than we want it ourselves. That's the mystery of love.

30 *"Where I am you also may be."*
(Jn 14:3)

This promise of Jesus is partially fulfilled at the time of our own baptism when Jesus comes invisibly to abide with us through the Holy Spirit dwelling with us. In this life our experiential awareness of the presence of Jesus is only sporadic.

When you love someone with your whole heart, you come more fully alive when in that person's presence. This is also true when we are aware of the presence of Jesus. Heaven is a state of total immersion in the trinitarian love.

"Now we see indistinctly, as in a mirror; then we shall see face to face" (1 Cor 13:12).

31 *"You know the way that leads where I go."*
(Jn 14:4)

Jesus incorporated the essence of his teaching in the beatitudes, which he lived himself. His life challenges our emulation.

"What I just did was to give you an example: / as I have done, so must you do." (Jn 13:15)

"Learn from me, for I am gentle and humble of heart." (Mt 11:29)

"Show me, O Lord, your way, and lead me on a level path." (Ps 27:11)

Believe Me!
Rejoice in Hope!

THIS MONTH WE WILL be reflecting on two of the three theological virtues: faith and hope. These virtues are basic to our spiritual growth and maturation since they have God as their object.

During the first twelve days we will concentrate on the virtue of faith as found in various passages of sacred scripture. Throughout his earthly sojourn, Jesus pleaded for an unwavering faith in him and in his Father. He wants us to have a committed faith that enables us to say yes to the Lord at all times. Our expectant faith assures us that God will respond to our need in every situation.

For the next thirteen days our focus will be on the Lord and his extravagant promises to us. Such a focus generates a fervent hope in our hearts. God is always and everywhere the object of our hope. Our dependence on the Lord will increase the hope within us.

In the last six reflections for this month we meet Jesus on the sea (Mt 14:22-33). In this episode Jesus reminds us that we should step out in faith and hope at all times, even in the midst of a tempest. He promises to come to our rescue just as he did for Peter, provided, like Peter, we keep our focus in his direction and not in the direction of some false security.

This reassurance gives a lilt to our journeying. Life becomes a happy excursion with Jesus into the loving arms of our Father.

1 *"Blest are they who have not seen and have believed."* (Jn 20:29)

Often we struggle with something we cannot see or understand. Our intellect wants proof. Yet our minds are too limited to grasp the divine. This calls for blind faith. Only our hearts can assure us that it is credible. This is the kind of faith which pleased Jesus so many times in the gospel and down through the ages since. For this kind of faith he promises special blessings.

2 *"I do not pray for them alone. / I pray also for those who will believe in me through their word."* (Jn 17:20)

In his high-priestly prayer, Jesus prayed that every person who heard the disciples proclaim his word would believe in him. He also prayed that the radiant faith of the disciples would draw many to him.

Jesus prays today that those who hear the good news through our words and our lifestyle may be humble and open of heart to believe and follow him. May our vibrant faith be a compelling, magnetic power drawing many to the feet of Jesus!

3 *"I assure you, if you had faith the size of a mustard seed, you would be able to say to this mountain, 'Move from here to there' and it would move."* (Mt 17:20)

In Hebrew parlance the word mountain stands for any difficulty or hardship we encounter. Jesus assures us that a dynamic, operative faith will enable us to remove or surmount all hardships and difficulties. Even the hardest tasks can be accomplished. A deep, abiding faith lightens our burden and makes our journey a joyous, jubilant pilgrimage.

Lord, increase my faith!

4 *"I am the resurrection and the life; / whoever believes in me, / though he should die, will come to life; / and whoever is alive and believes in me / will never die."* (Jn 11:25-26)

By his death and resurrection Jesus redeemed our fallen human nature, giving it the potential to share in his risen, exalted life. Our sharing in this life is only partial because of our human limitation.

As we go through the portals of death, Jesus meets us and endows us with an outpouring of his divine life, thus uniting us in a rich, personal union of love with himself, with the Father, and with the Holy Spirit.

He stands on his word.

5 *"Did I not assure you that if you believed you would see the glory of God displayed?"*
(Jn 11:40)

Jesus was not only speaking to Martha in these words, but to all of us down through the ages. To see the glory of God we must stand in wonder at a gorgeous sunset, in reverence at the birth of a baby, in awe at the dexterity of our own hands.

Just as his divine love is without limit, so the manifestation of his love is endless. With the eyes of faith, we can see the glory of God at every turn in the road.

6 *"If you do not believe / when I tell you about earthly things, / how are you to believe / when I tell you about those of heaven?"* (Jn 3:12)

Our rational minds cannot grasp or understand many of the mysteries we encounter in our mundane existence. We must rely on the word of some educated authority.

Jesus asks for that same credibility, not only when he reveals earthly things, but especially when he tells us about heavenly things. Have we any greater authority or a more trustworthy witness?

7 *For if you confess with your lips that Jesus is the Lord, and believe in your heart that God raised him from the dead, you will be saved.* (Rom 10:9)

Faith means not only intellectually accepting a truth which we cannot understand, but it means making a commitment. If we believe so convincingly in a truth or cause that we are willing to devote our time, talent, and energy to it, we are living a committed faith. The vowed life in marriage or the religious life requires an even greater faith of commitment. If our commitment to Jesus as Lord is equally strong, we will be saved because our whole way of living will be geared to that end.

8 *"And you," he said to them, "who do you say that I am?"* (Mt 16:15)

At first the answer to this question seems quite obvious, yet it merits our consideration and response. Is Jesus my first thought in the morning when I awaken, my constant companion at work or play throughout the day, my first recourse in trials and troubles? Do my thoughts turn often to him in praise and gratitude, in reverence and honor?

9 *"What little sense you have! How slow you are to believe."* (Lk 24:25)

Jesus certainly was sympathetic with the two disciples on the road to Emmaus who were discouraged and dejected. Yet he wanted to point out to them that it was their lack of faith which caused their disappointment. First, he chided them and then revealed himself to them after explaining how all the scriptures were fulfilled in him.

As we travel the road of life, we may find ourselves despondent and discouraged at times. Perhaps it is due to our lack of faith.

10 *"Unless you people see signs and wonders, you do not believe."* (Jn 4:48)

How often a doubting Thomas attitude arises within us! It may not be that a certain truth baffles our minds, as much as the assertion is simply not to our liking. If we receive sufficient "signs and wonders," we may be willing to listen or even to change our minds.

Jesus says to us as he did to Thomas: "Do not persist in your unbelief, but believe!" (Jn 20:27).

Lord, I do believe! Help my unbelief!

11 *He could work no miracle there, apart from curing a few who were sick by laying hands on them, so much did their lack of faith distress him.* (Mk 6:5-6)

Jesus is a patient God who waits. He does not force himself upon us. He waits for us to accept him in faith, to invite him into our lives, even though we cannot comprehend his divine plans for us.

The citizens of Nazareth, his hometown, did not benefit from his healing ministry because of their lack of faith which distressed him. His divine works in our midst are contingent, likewise, upon our acceptance of him in faith.

12 *"My Lord and my God!"* (Jn 20:28)

After Thomas wrestled with his doubts and the fear that perhaps the news that Jesus was alive was just too good to be true, he made one of the briefest and most moving professions of faith: "My Lord and my God!"

With Thomas, down through the ages we, too, renew our own faith by repeating his memorable words: "My Lord and my God!"

13 *"She [Mary] is to have a son and you are to name him Jesus because he will save his people from their sins."* (Mt 1:21)

Our Christian era was inaugurated with great hope and expectancy. The angel's message to us through Joseph is most reassuring: "he will save his people from their sins."

We are "his people" when we come to him admitting our sinfulness and our need for his forgiving, healing love.

Be merciful to me a sinner, O Lord!

14 *The grace of God has appeared, offering salvation to all men. It trains us to reject godless ways and worldly desires, and live temperately, justly, and devoutly in this age as we await our blessed hope, the appearing of the glory of the great God and of our Savior Christ Jesus.* (Ti 2:11-13)

We cannot save ourselves without God's help. Paul set us straight on this: "It is owing to his favor that salvation is yours through faith" (Eph 2:8). A dynamic, operative faith of commitment will enable us to live "temperately, justly, and devoutly."

15 *"I have come to call, not the self-righteous, but sinners."* (Mt 9:13)

Jesus never lost sight of his redemptive mission. He associated with sinners. He loved them. He even ate with them, which was a taboo in those times. In attempting to justify themselves, the self-righteous were not open to receive his redemptive love.

We need to regularly assess our own disposition toward Christ.

16 *You must hold fast to faith, be firmly grounded and steadfast in it, unshaken in the hope promised you by the gospel you have heard.* (Col 1:23)

The gospel is an inexhaustible source of hope for us. Its message portrays God's infinite love for us—a love that counts every hair on our head, a love that fulfills all his promises. Can there be any greater source of hope than this?

17 *Let us hold unswervingly to our profession which gives us hope, for he who made the promise deserves our trust.* (Heb 10:23)

When doubts, fears, anxieties, and misgivings arise in our daily living, we need to ask ourselves what other alternatives we have on our journey through life.

After a momentary reflection we can say with Peter: "Lord, to whom shall we go? You have the words of eternal life" (Jn 6:68). Thus hope springs eternal!

18 *May our Lord Jesus Christ himself, may God our Father who loved us and in his mercy gave us eternal consolation and hope, console your hearts and strengthen them for every good work and word.* (2 Thes 2:16-17)

These inspired words leave no place for discouragement in our lives. Our heavenly Father is "the God of all consolation!" Our hope greatly increases as we reflect on Paul's message: "He comforts us in all our afflictions and thus enables us to comfort those who are in trouble, with the same consolation we have received from him" (2 Cor 1:4).

19 *May he enlighten your innermost vision that you may know the great hope to which he has called you, the wealth of his glorious heritage to be distributed among the members of the Church.* (Eph 1:18)

Hope is one of the great gifts of the Holy Spirit. Hope enables us to set a goal in life. With the enlightenment of the Holy Spirit, we are able to pursue a way of life leading to that goal—our glorious heritage.

Hope increases as we step out in trust. It spurs us on in moments of doubt and hesitation.

20 *Rejoice in hope, be patient under trial, persevere in prayer.* (Rom 12:12)

A person without hope will suffer depression, disappointment, discouragement. On the other hand, hope will raise our focus above the changes and challenges of life to a peace and joy which the world cannot give.

In all of this we can hear Jesus say to us: "Trust me."

21 *Like a sure and firm anchor, that hope extends beyond the veil through which Jesus, our forerunner, has entered on our behalf, being made high priest forever according to the order of Melchizedek.* (Heb 6:19)

The anchor has been a long-standing symbol of hope. An anchor can hold a ship stationary; otherwise the waves and swells would cause it to flounder about aimlessly.

Jesus is our hope when the winds and waves of life buffet us. Regardless of the intensity of the storms, our hope is firmly rooted in Jesus, who never leaves us, but is with us at every moment and in every circumstance.

22 *We know that affliction makes for endurance, and endurance for tested virtue, and tested virtue for hope. And this hope will not leave us disappointed.* (Rom 5:3-5)

There is an aura of mystery surrounding suffering, yet one of the usual fruits is a peaceful, even joyous acceptance. As we accept affliction, we are better able to endure it. These dispositions all spring from the virtue of hope. From our own experience we must agree with Paul that this hope will never leave us disappointed. Hope brings true happiness in our lives.

23 *I cannot even understand my own actions. I do not do what I want to do but what I hate.... What a wretched man I am! Who can free me from this body under the power of death? All praise to God, through Jesus Christ our Lord!* (Rom 7:15, 24-25)

In this reflection Paul meditates on the weakness of our human nature. When he says, "no good dwells in me," he means that the blessing of salvation comes not from us, but from God. As we recognize the sinfulness of our human nature, we join with Paul in praising God for the gift of his Son Jesus as our Savior and Redeemer.

24 *"It is the will of him who sent me / that I should lose nothing of what he has given me; / rather, that I should raise it up on the last day."* (Jn 6:39)

What hope this solemn promise of Jesus inspires in us! Both Jesus and the Father want us to be raised "up on the last day" and to bask in the trinitarian love for all eternity.

In the Holy Eucharist Jesus is not only our Companion but our food for the journey as well.

25 *We would have you be clear about those who sleep in death, brothers; otherwise you might yield to grief like those who have no hope. For if we believe that Jesus died and rose, God will bring forth with him from the dead those who have fallen asleep believing in him.*

(1 Thes 4:13-14)

By redeeming our fallen human nature, Jesus was able to share his risen, glorified life with us, but only partially, because of our limited capacity to receive it.

Death is the doorway enabling us to share more fully in his divine life and love. This is the union for which Jesus prayed: "That they may be one, as we are one" (Jn 17:22).

Jesus Walks on the Water

Meanwhile the boat, already several hundred yards out from the shore, was being tossed about in the waves raised by strong headwinds. At about three in the morning, he came walking toward them on the lake. When the disciples saw him walking on the water, they were terrified. "It is a ghost!" they said, and in their fear they began to cry out. Jesus hastened to reassure them: "Get hold of yourselves! It is I. Do not be afraid!" Peter spoke up and said, "Lord, if it is really you, tell me to come to you across the water." "Come!" he said. So Peter got out of the boat and began to walk on the water, moving toward Jesus. But when he perceived how strong the wind was, he became frightened and began to sink as he cried out, "Lord, save me!" Jesus at once stretched out his hand and caught him. "How little faith you have!" he exclaimed. "Why did you falter?" (Mt 14:24-31)

26 *"Get hold of yourselves! It is I. Do not be afraid."* (Mt 14:27)

When the Lord manifests his presence and power in our lives, it may momentarily surprise and frighten us. When the Lord manifests his divine intervention in the gospel, we hear the words: "Do not be afraid." When a task seems impossible, when a pain is particularly sharp, when a disappointment pierces deeply, when the road seems rough and rocky, we need to pause to listen in prayer as Jesus says to us: "It is I. Do not be afraid."

27 *"Lord, if it is really you, tell me to come to you across the water."* (Mt 14:28)

Peter wanted to be close to Jesus because he loved him. He did not calculate the risk involved. This incident gave Jesus an opportunity to teach Peter and us a valuable lesson on trust. When we keep ourselves aware that Jesus is always with us, we will be encouraged to take risks. To live close to Jesus we must dare to be different. This is the commitment which Jesus asks of us.

28 *"Come!"* (Mt 14:29)

This simple, direct invitation coming from the lips of Jesus is addressed to us each day. Come follow him. Come walk in his footsteps. Come walk so closely to him that we can be identified with him. This is our mission in life: to put on the Lord Jesus and radiate him to all we meet.

29 *"Lord, save me!"* (Mt 14:30)

Peter had no difficulty walking on the water until he became frightened and began to doubt Jesus' invitation, "Come!" Note that Peter did not turn back and struggle to get back into the boat, but he kept his eyes fixed on Jesus. If we keep our eyes riveted on Jesus at all times we, too, will be able to do the extraordinary. Trust him!

30 *Jesus at once stretched out his hand and caught him.* (Mt 14:31)

When Peter began to sink as he attempted to come to Jesus over the water, he cried out for help, "Lord, save me!" Jesus at once reached out to rescue him. We can be assured as we strive to come to Jesus and recognize our need for his help, that he will immediately stretch out his hand to us. Jesus says simply, "Trust me!"

31 *"How little faith you have! Why did you falter?"* (Mt 14:31)

Few things please Jesus more than a deep, abiding faith in him. When we believe firmly enough in him to trust him, to commit ourselves to him, he is greatly pleased with our faith.

Our faith may be tested at times. When the winds of life blow violently against us, when the cresting waves threaten to engulf us, our confident cry, "Lord, save us!" will not only please Jesus greatly, but it will bring an immediate rescuing response to our need.

Do You Love Me?

N O THEOLOGICAL TREATISE is more concise, yet more comprehensive than John's proclamation: "God is love" (1 Jn 4:16). Love awaits a response because by its nature love is mutual.

In the first week's proposed scriptures, Jesus instructs us to what extent we are to respond in love. The intensity and the fidelity of our response will determine the degree of our happiness in this life and in the life to come.

In the second week we turn to the pastoral teachings of Paul as our guide. In a few masterfully chosen words, he gives us a classic description of the qualities inherent in Christian love. Jesus manifested these characteristics to an eminent degree. As his followers, we are committed to strive toward this standard of love in our daily ministry.

For the third week we turn to John who writes a beautiful love letter. Love letters are a special kind of communication. We treasure them; we read and reread them. In his love letter John teaches us some important and practical truths about love. Letting his words inspire us each day will bring us to a richer appreciation of God's love for us and our love for him.

For our prayer time toward the end of the month we meet Jesus in the sacred precincts of the temple expounding on how much we must love the Lord our God and our neighbor. Jesus raises our vision above any and all limits as he challenges us to love with all our heart, with all our soul, with all our mind, and with all our strength.

1 *I love you, O Lord, my strength, / O Lord, my rock, my fortress, my deliverer. / My God, my rock of refuge, / my shield, the horn of my salvation, my stronghold.* (Ps 18:2-3)

The psalmist realizes that God is the source of all that is good in his life. Words cannot express the immensity of God's love. He uses various images to describe what cannot be put into words.

In the same way, God lavishes his love upon us—providentially, forgivingly, enduringly. He surrounds us with his beauty. He envelops us in the joy and warmth of his love.

As we contemplate his love during these coming days, we are loving him in return.

2 *"There is no greater love than this: / to lay down one's life for one's friends."* (Jn 15:13)

Jesus is always our model and exemplar. He set the pace for us and bids us to follow him. Jesus not only told us that our love should be so great that we should be willing to lay down our lives for a loved one, but he proved his love for us by laying down his own life the very next day.

Thank you, Jesus, for loving me so much!

3 *"It was not you who chose me, / it was I who chose you / to go forth and bear fruit."*

(Jn 15:16)

Jesus first taught us how much we must love. Then he chose us to be apostles of love. This is the fruit we are to bear. Jesus fills us with his own love, then he reaches out through us to love others. This is our special calling—to permit him to love us, to let him love others through us, and to love others with Jesus.

4 *"This is my commandment: / love one another / as I have loved you."* (Jn 15:12)

Love is the hallmark of our Christian way of life. It was said of the early Christians, "See how they love one another." Our love must reach out to God, to our neighbor, and to ourselves. Jesus tells us how much we must love: "as I have loved you." That standard may seem like an impossible goal. However, Jesus would never have set it if it were not achievable. Jesus looks at our intentions. Do we want to love as much as he loved us? If so, we are beginning to achieve the goal he set for us.

5 *"You shall love your neighbor as yourself."* (Mt 22:39)

This commandment is difficult for most of us simply because we do not love ourselves as we ought. If we are insecure, if our self-image is rather low, it will be difficult for us to reach out in love to others. We are so fragile. We do not want to be rejected. We hesitate to make ourselves vulnerable.

On the other hand, when we know that we are loved and that we are lovable, then we will want to reach out with more loving concern for others. Love needs to be shared in order to grow and mature.

6 *"The command I give you is this, / that you love one another."* (Jn 15:17)

This directive of Jesus is unmistakably clear. How to achieve this goal is a major concern of ours. We need to recall that the Holy Spirit is the very source of love, and we are his temple. He is abiding with us and within us. As we strive to be receptive to the influx of his love, we are reaching out in love to others. We must let him love us, so that we can love others.

7 *"My command to you is: love your enemies, pray for your persecutors."* (Mt 5:44)

This command of Jesus may be a shocker at first. When we realize that he is living within us, filling us with his own divine love, then it becomes easier for us to permit him to channel his love through us to those we consider enemies.

In due time this kind of love will claim many an enemy as a friend. Nothing will make us more Christlike. He says, "As I have done, so you must do" (Jn 13:15).

8 *Love is patient.* (1 Cor 13:4)

John Chrysostom said that patient people are those who are wronged and who have it in their power to avenge themselves, and yet they will not do so. Jesus was patient in dealing with his slow-to-believe disciples and even with his enemies, whom he could have devastated. Such patience is not a sign of weakness, but of strength. It is not defeatism, but rather the way to victory.

Jesus was patient; so ought we to be patient.

9 *Love is kind.* (1 Cor 13:4)

Jerome called kindness the benignity of love. A kind person is a gentle person, a considerate person. A kind person thinks first of others. Such a person has a sympathetic nature. Such a person automatically radiates kindness and consideration for others.

Jesus invites us to be gentle. "Learn from me for I am gentle and humble of heart" (Mt 11:29).

10 *Love is not jealous.* (1 Cor 1:4)

A jealous person is an unhappy person. He or she also brings misery to others. A jealous person is fearful of losing another's exclusive devotion. Such a person is always distrustful and suspicious.

On the other hand if we love, we trust the person we love implicitly. We are never suspicious of them. We want to share them with others. Jesus shared his mother with us. He brought us to the Father. He was not exclusive.

11 *It does not put on airs, it is not snobbish.*
(1 Cor 13:4)

Genuine love could never tolerate putting on airs, because persons loved are usually humbled by the consciousness that they are loved. Likewise, real love is never snobbish, because a real lover feels that he or she is never quite good enough for the beloved. On the other hand snobs tend to rebuff anyone they consider inferior in matters of knowledge or taste.

12 *Love is never rude, it is not self-seeking.*
(1 Cor 13:5)

Rudeness is a lack of consideration for others—their feelings, their opinions, and their rights. In contrast, there is a graciousness in Christian love that never forgets that courtesy, tact, and politeness are expressions and manifestations of love.

Self-seeking is not a component part of love. Many of life's problems would be solved if we thought less of our privileges and rights and more of our duties and responsibilities.

How simply Jesus stated it: "Love your neighbor as yourself."

13 *It is not prone to anger, neither does it brood over injuries.* (1 Cor 13:5)

Anger is a strong feeling or reaction of displeasure toward others. Christlike love never becomes exasperated with people. Exasperation is always a sign of weakness and insecurity. The person who masters his temper is the person who loves as Jesus loved.

Jesus' anger at the buyers and sellers in the temple was righteous indignation at the disgraceful desecration of this sacred place of worship.

14 *There is no limit to love's forbearance, to its trust, its hope, its power to endure.*
(1 Cor 13:7)

Love proves its forbearance by accepting the faults and mistakes of others. Love takes God at his word and trusts him. Love also trusts other people. By trusting another person completely, we may make him trustworthy.

By his loving concern for others, Jesus proved that no one was hopeless. Thus he loved. Love has the power to endure all things not merely with passive resignation, but with triumphant fortitude, knowing that a caring God is watching over us.

15 *"Have no love for the world, / nor the things that the world affords. / If anyone loves the world, / the Father's love has no place in him."*
(1 Jn 2:15)

There is a great dichotomy between worldly standards and God's standards. Let Jesus explain it:

> No man can serve two masters. He will either hate one and love the other or be attentive to one and despise the other. You cannot give yourself to God and money. (Mt 6:24)

The psalmist put it this way: "Happy the man who follows not / the counsel of the wicked . . . / but delights in the law of the Lord" (Ps 1:1-2).

16 *The way we came to understand love / was that he laid down his life for us; / we too must lay down our lives for our brothers.*
(1 Jn 3:16)

Jesus always gave us the example first before he asked us to follow. We may never be led off to martyrdom or crucifixion, but we are often called upon to die to self by accommodating ourselves to the wishes or needs of others. Love will help us make this dying to self gentle and gradual.

17 *Let us love one another / because love is of God; / everyone who loves is begotten of God / and has knowledge of God.* (1 Jn 4:7)

We cannot love God if we do not know him. We come to know him as he reveals himself to us in the quiet prayer of listening. This knowledge of the heart helps us to understand how we share in his divine life and love. Then we comprehend in a small way how we are "begotten of God." Jesus redeemed us and the Father adopted us as his daughters and sons.

18 *Love, then, consists in this: / not that we have loved God / but that he has loved us / and has sent his Son as an offering for our sins.* (1 Jn 4:10)

We often have the feeling that we must merit or earn God's love for us. On the contrary, God's love for us is so great that he created us even before we were able to love him.

To assure us of that unmerited love, Jesus willingly poured out his life on the cross for our salvation—effecting our union with him in love. The return he asks of us is a response in loving praise and thanksgiving.

19 *No one has ever seen God. Yet if we love one another / God dwells in us, / and his love is brought to perfection in us.* (1 Jn 4:12)

Today people want to see God, to know him by experiencing his love and his presence. As we permit the Lord to love us, our actions and attitudes will reflect the love, peace, and joy which only he can give. This is how we and others will be able to know God. Thus his love will be brought into perfection in us.

20 *God is love, / and he who abides in love / abides in God / and God in him.* (1 Jn 4:16)

In baptism we are made divine. The Holy Spirit, the source and essence of divine love, makes of each one of us his temple. He is dynamic and operative within us purifying and sanctifying us as he abides with us. "All who are led by the Spirit of God are sons of God. . . . The Spirit himself gives witness with our spirit that we are children of God" (Rom 8:14ff).

What a dignity is ours as Christians—Christ-bearers!

21 *Love has no room for fear; / rather, perfect love casts out all fear.* (1 Jn 4:18)

Love trusts to the hilt. Love convinces us that the Lord does forgive our sins and that he wants us to be united with him in heaven even more than we could want it ourselves. This knowledge generates a more perfect love in us and eliminates all fear. This is the mystery of God who is love.

22 *"Simon, son of John, do you love me more than these?"* (Jn 21:15)

At one time Peter boasted: "Though all may have their faith in you shaken, mine will never be shaken." Now Jesus asks Peter if he loves him more than the other disciples who also ran away when Jesus was arrested.

Like Peter, we, too, may profess our loyalty to and our love for Jesus, but in a moment of weakness or panic, we may also fail him. Jesus looks into your eyes and asks: "Do you love me more than these?"

23 *"Do you love me?"* (Jn 21:16)

Peter denied Jesus three times. Jesus restored his dignity when he gave Peter a triple opportunity to affirm his love.

After our falls, Jesus asks us again and again: "Do you love me?" Before we eagerly respond, let us test ourselves by asking ourselves if we see in every duty, in every joy and sorrow, in every demand made upon us a way of pleasing the Lord. We please the Lord by willingly, joyously, accepting whatever he permits to come our way.

24 *"Do you love me?"* (Jn 21:17)

Love is a great privilege, but it brings with it a great responsibility. We love Jesus by loving others. Love must be translated into action.

Jesus asks us again if we love him, because loving makes us vulnerable, and we must be willing to take the risk of being hurt if we truly love. This is the risk Jesus wants us to take when he says: "Feed my lambs. Tend my sheep."

No one loved more than Jesus did. No one was more vulnerable. No one was hurt more severely.

The Greatest Commandment

"Which is the first of all the commandments?"
Jesus replied:
"This is the first:
   'Hear, O Israel! The Lord our God is Lord
      alone!
   Therefore you shall love the Lord your God
   with all your heart,
   with all your soul,
   with all your mind,
   and with all your strength.'
This is the second,
   'You shall love your neighbor as yourself.'"
                                    (Mk 12:28-31)

25 *"Hear, O Israel! The Lord our God is Lord alone!"* (Mk 12:29)

These words are known as the Shema, the creed of the Hebrews. The Jews recited it daily and affixed its words to the door of every home and every door within the home. It was also attached to their wrists and foreheads when they prayed.

Jesus set the stage for his solemn pronouncement on the two great commandments of love. The Shema served as a constant reminder of God's unfathomable love and people's duty to respond to the outpouring of his love.

We, too, need a constant reminder.

26 *"Therefore you shall love the Lord your God."* (Mk 12:30)

How succinctly John says that God first loved us, and to that love we owe our very existence. God's love for us is so infinite, so fathomless that we cannot grasp it with our finite minds. We need to dichotomize his love even to begin to grasp its implications. We speak of his creative, providential, forgiving, enduring love.

As the immensity of his love overwhelms us we can only respond: "Lord, I love you, too."

27 *"With all your heart."* (Mk 12:30)

Psychologists claim that we live more by our heart than by our head. When we experience the outpouring love of the Lord for us at every moment of the day, our heart wants to respond, because love, by its very nature, is mutual.

As we spend time in quiet, listening prayer, we will more readily experience his love for us. "You shall indeed find him when you search after him with your whole heart and your whole soul" (Dt 4:29).

28 *"With all your soul."* (Mk 12:30)

Our soul is our animating principle. It is our moving spirit. It is the actuating cause of all our thoughts, words, and deeds.

When we strive to love the Lord with our whole soul, we are loving at the very depth of our being. The fervor of our love is energized by our soul. Jesus explicitly mentioned our soul because he wanted to emphasize that there should be no limit to our response to the Father's love and his own love for each one of us.

29 *"With all your mind."* (Mk 12:30)

We cannot love a person we do not know. When we daily behold the beauty of God's creation, when we experience his providential care and concern for us, all of which springs from the fathomless fountain of his divine love, we cannot help responding in love.

Jesus said: "You will live in my love / if you keep my commandments" (Jn 15:10). He might have added: "It is the only way to true happiness here and hereafter."

30 *"And with all your strength."* (Mk 12:30)

Love is the dynamic of all our actions, "for it is love and love alone which makes the world go round."

Once we have experienced God's personal love for us, we want to respond with every fiber of our being. When God becomes our first priority, then we will strain every muscle to express our love with all our strength. Love urges us to heights and depths which otherwise we would never attempt. Love never counts the cost.

31 *"This is the second, / 'You shall love your neighbor as yourself.'"* (Mk 12:31)

This second part of the great commandment follows naturally from the first. If we love God as our kind, faithful Father, then we will find it easier to love our neighbor. Our neighbor, like ourselves, is an adopted daughter or son of our heavenly Father. Jesus is not only our Brother, but also a Brother of our neighbor. That makes us family, children of God, people of God, the body of Christ.

Jesus Prayed

THIS MONTH WE ARE CONCENTRATING on the prayer of Jesus. Did Jesus pray always? How did Jesus pray? What does Jesus teach us by his example?

For the first few days of this month, we contemplate the prayer of Jesus as he prayed communally with others, as he prayed liturgically with his people.

As we continue to listen to the suggested scriptural passages, we discover that Jesus consistently set aside time for formal prayer. He also prayed everywhere and always in the midst of his demanding ministry. He prayed on the job—on location if you will. Throughout his public life Jesus would pause momentarily to raise his mind and heart to his Father in fervent prayer. As we reflect with Jesus on some of these occasions, we will be encouraged to do the same in our daily round of duties.

Third, we discover that Jesus was a contemplative in action. Today the Lord is calling us to be active contemplatives in the world. Contemplative prayer is a powerful antidote in our materialistic, humanistic society. It gives us "insights beyond analysis."

We will learn to pray contemplatively as we accompany Jesus as he prayed "in seclusion," as "he was absorbed in prayer," as he spent "the night in communion with God." In the closing days of this month, we will meditate on the prayer which Jesus himself taught us—the Lord's Prayer.

1 *One day he was praying in a certain place.*
When he had finished one of his disciples
asked him, *"Lord, teach us to pray."* (Lk 11:1)

Prayer consists in a mutual giving. In
prayer we give ourselves to God. We give
him our time; we try to set aside the
preoccupations of our daily routine. In
return God gives us an awareness of his
presence, an experience of his love. We feel
a peace and joy, a consolation and com-
panionship which only he can give. For
this we humbly pray: "Lord, teach us to
pray."

2 *Entering the synagogue on the sabbath as he*
was in the habit of doing. (Lk 4:16)

Jesus went regularly to the synagogue to
follow the ritual of his people and also to
pray with them. By his own example Jesus
showed us the importance and the necessity of praying liturgically as a community.
Praying liturgically is a public profession
of faith. When we pray as a community, it
gives greater honor and glory, greater
praise and thanks to our glorious Father in
heaven. Praying together is a matrix, a
powerful unifying force welding us together as God's family.

3 *"Did you not know I had to be in my Father's house?"* (Lk 2:49)

The will of the Father was always the first priority in the life of Jesus. He needed to remain in the Father's house of prayer at this time, even though he knew it would cause his mother pain and distress.

Fulfilling our duty to our heavenly Father may cost us some discipline, some inconvenience, some dying to self, perhaps even some misunderstanding, but like Jesus we need to put first things first. Therein we will find great consolation.

4 *"Do this as a remembrance of me."* (Lk 22:19)

Jesus gave us the greatest of all liturgical prayers when he instituted the Eucharist. It derives its power from the fact that Jesus is the principal celebrant. He invites us to join him in praising and thanking his Father and ours.

Jesus transforms the gift of ourselves, represented by the bread and wine, into himself, thus giving our gift an infinite dimension acceptable to the Father. No other prayer can be more powerful, more praiseworthy, more pleasing to God, and it is our daily privilege.

5 *Once he had arrived at the house, he permitted no one to enter with him except Peter,
John, James, and the child's parents.* (Lk 8:51)

Jesus knew the power in group prayer.
He wanted the prayer-support of his three
favorite apostles when he went to restore
life to the daughter of Jairus. Jesus gave us
this example with the hope that we might
seek the support of the prayers of others
when we face difficult situations. He continues to remind us: "Where two or three
are gathered in my name, there am I in their
midst" (Mt 18:20).

6 *He took Peter, John and James, and went up
onto a mountain to pray.* (Lk 9:28)

Jesus practiced shared prayer with
others, especially with his favorite prayer-
team: Peter, James, and John. Jesus also
prayed before all the important events of
his life. He went up to Mt. Tabor to discern
the Father's will concerning his going up to
Jerusalem to begin his ministry of suffering. Prayer enabled Jesus to say yes to the
Father. He was supported in this resolve
by his prayer-team.

7 *He took along Peter and Zebedee's two sons, and began to experience sorrow and distress.*
(Mt 26:37)

In times of great affliction we find much comfort and consolation when those dear to us are present with us. Their presence and their prayers are a powerful, comforting, healing support. In his darkest hour Jesus taught us this valuable lesson of calling upon family and friends for their prayerful presence. We need to remember, too, that Jesus is always with us as our comforter and consoler.

8 *One day when Jesus was praying in seclusion and his disciples were with him, he put the question to them, "Who do the crowds say that I am?"* (Lk 9:18)

Spending time alone with the Lord in prayer gives us insights, wisdom, and understanding beyond our intellectual comprehension. It was during prayer that Jesus asked for a profession of faith in himself. In prayer Peter recognized him as "the Messiah of God."

In prayer we will come to know Jesus as a personal, loving Lord abiding with us always. We cannot arrive at this deeper, richer knowledge of him without prayer.

9 *Jesus then took the loaves of bread, gave thanks and passed them around to those reclining there.* (Jn 6:11)

With the famished crowd pressing upon him, Jesus took time calmly and serenely to thank his Father for his loving care and concern for these pilgrim-people. This is how Jesus prayed on location.

Busyness besets us daily. Jesus shows us how to pray in the midst of all the daily demands. A momentary prayer interspersed throughout the day will help us physically, emotionally, and spiritually.

10 *On one occasion Jesus spoke thus: "Father, Lord of heaven and earth, to you I offer praise; for what you have hidden from the learned and the clever you have revealed to the merest children."* (Mt 11:25)

There is ample proof that Jesus prayed always and everywhere. He paused in his demanding schedule to praise and thank the Father for revealing the mysteries of heaven to humble, simple souls. Jesus was so pleased with the faith and trust of his hearers that he stopped to express his thanks and praise. Like Jesus, we want to sprinkle our day with little prayers of thanks and petitions to our providing Father!

11 *"Father, I thank you for having heard me."*
(Jn 11:41)

Jesus frequently showed us by his own example how important our sense of gratitude is. With a hushed, curious, crowd surrounding him and in an atmosphere charged with expectancy, Jesus paused at the grave of Lazarus to raise his thoughts far above his mundane surroundings to his Father in heaven. "Father, I thank you."

Gratitude will strengthen our faith and trust. "Father, I, too, thank you for this present moment and for this insight."

12 *"For these I pray— / not for the world / but for those you have given me, / for they are really yours."* (Jn 17:9)

In his great high-priestly prayer, Jesus prayed for each one of us. He prayed that we might not only accept the gospel message, but that we would proclaim it by our own lifestyle. This is our mission in life. We will never know when our attitudes, our reaction, and our behavior may touch someone. We might well ask ourselves: "What have I done this day to prove that I am a Christian?"

13 *"I pray also for those who believe in me through their word, / that all may be one / as you, Father are in me and I in you; / I pray that they may be one in us."* (Jn 17:20)

Jesus prays that we might be united with him and the Father and the Holy Spirit in that community of perfect love, the Holy Trinity. There can be no greater optimum, no greater gift, no greater blessing. May our daily response be: "To do your will, O my God, is my delight" (Ps 40:9).

14 *"That all may be one / as you, Father, are in me, and I in you; / I pray that they may be one in us, / that the world may believe that you sent me."* (Jn 17:21)

There is no unifying force more powerful than praying together with others and for others. Nor is there any prayer more effective than the prayer of Jesus. Jesus prayed that we might become one with him and with the Father. As we pray, we will become more receptive and more pliable to the Lord's transforming power. Prayer will form the mind and heart of Jesus in us.

15 *He went down on his knees and prayed in these words: "Father, if it is your will, take this cup from me; yet not my will but yours be done." (Lk 22:41-42)*

In this dreadful moment of his agony, Jesus' whole human nature cringed at the prospect of what lay ahead—the excruciating physical pain, the revolting rejection, the shame and disgrace which he had to endure. In spite of all this Jesus was willing to accept the Father's plan for our redemption.

Jesus' prayer is the source of our strength and acceptance of God's will in our lives. With his grace we can say, "Thy will be done."

16 *"Father forgive them; they do not know what they are doing." (Lk 23:34)*

What more memorable instance have we of Jesus praying on location than this prayerful, compassionate plea from his deathbed on the cross? In this hour of agonizing pain he was praying for us.

Even in moments of suffering we can whisper a prayer for others. Our focus on Jesus will diminish our own pain and add power to our prayer. At these moments, if words do not come, only a thought or our intention is sufficient.

17 *He often retired to deserted places and prayed.* (Lk 5:16)

Jesus did not pray intermittently, or when the occasion arose, or when time permitted. Jesus made time for prayer. He prayed consistently and regularly. If we are to make progress in our union with the Lord, we need to discipline ourselves so that we, too, have time for prayer. The time spent with the Lord in prayer will enrich and deepen our love relationship with him. Keeping a journal of the time we spend with the Lord each day is a helpful means for progressing in prayer.

18 *When all the people were baptized, and Jesus was at prayer after likewise being baptized, the sky opened and the Holy Spirit descended on him in a visible form like a dove.* (Lk 3:21)

After Jesus had taken this initial step into his public ministry, he wanted to be alone with his Father to ascertain the next step in his public ministry. While Jesus was at prayer, the Holy Spirit came upon him to guide and direct him while the Father confirmed his mission: "You are my beloved Son. On you my favor rests" (Lk 3:22).

19 *When he had taken leave of them, he went off to the mountain to pray.* (Mk 6:46)

How often the scriptures remind us that whenever possible Jesus slipped away from the crowd to be alone with his Father in prayer. He showed us the necessity of being alone with the Lord in prayer to avoid fatigue and burnout and also to find encouragement and strength to accept the everyday trials. How clearly Jesus marked the pathway for us to follow.

20 *One day when Jesus was praying in seclusion.* (Lk 9:18)

Statements such as this are often in the gospel as gentle reminders that we, like Jesus, need to be alone with God from time to time. A quiet time, a holy hour, a day of prayer, or time spent on a retreat offer us such occasions to be alone with our loving Father and with Jesus. Jesus invites us: "Come by yourselves to an out-of-the-way place and rest a little" (Mk 6:31).

21 *In his anguish he prayed with all the greater intensity.* (Lk 22:44)

In the garden of Gethsemane, Jesus really struggled to say yes to the Father, since he foresaw all the horrible suffering which lay ahead. Because of the severity of this inner conflict, Jesus prayed "with all the greater intensity." In his prayer he found the courage, the strength, the fortitude to say: "Father, your will be done."

22 *Rising early the next morning, he went off to a lonely place in the desert; there he was absorbed in prayer.* (Mk 1:35)

Jesus prayed contemplatively. After a day of teaching and healing all who were brought to him, Jesus sought the isolation and privacy of the desert to be alone with the Father. Here he was "absorbed in prayer."

Our own absorption in prayer may bring us to an experience of the presence and love of the Lord. Our busy schedule may require us to rise early as Jesus did.

23 *Then he went out to the mountain to pray, spending the night in communion with God.* (Lk 6:12)

Jesus spent time in the prayer of listening: listening with his heart, listening at the depth of his being. The evangelist describes this kind of prayer as "communion with God."

Our attitude before the Lord must also be: "Here I am, Lord, what is it you want of me today?" or "What do you want to say to me today, Lord?" This kind of prayer will transform our minds and hearts to be more closely conformed with the mentality of Jesus.

24 *"Master, how good it is for us to be here."* (Lk 9:33)

These words were spoken by Peter on Mt. Tabor when he was overwhelmed by the divine splendor of Jesus radiating through his humanity. In the quiet time of prayer Jesus favors us with deeper insights into himself. We see more clearly his splendor and majesty, his loving concern and great compassion. In prayer, we, too, can say: "How good it is for us to be here."

The Lord's Prayer

This is how you are to pray:
Our Father in heaven,
hallowed be your name,
your kingdom come,
your will be done
on earth as it is in heaven.
Give us today our daily bread,
and forgive us the wrong we have done
as we forgive whose who wrong us.
Subject us not to the trial
but deliver us from the evil one.
(Mt 6:9-13)

25 *"Our Father in heaven."* (Mt 6:9)

Jesus taught us to call God, Father. This was a radical departure from the custom of that day. To the Jew the name of God was very sacred, and great care had to be taken to use that name reverently. Jesus went even farther. In this prayer he bids us to say, "Our Father." Since this was the only time in scripture that Jesus used the name "Our Father," I wonder if he were not implying that he was praying with us.

26 *"Hallowed be your name."* (Mt 6:9)

In this brief petition of the Lord's Prayer we ask that the name of God be held in esteem, duly honored and greatly respected. In biblical usage a name stands for the whole person. Thus we pray that the Lord be loved, adored, and worshiped in our own hearts and in the hearts of all people.

Hallow his name today!

27 *"Your kingdom come."* (Mt 6:10)

God's kingdom is a spiritual kingdom within us. We are his kingdom because the Holy Spirit has made us his temple and is dwelling within us with his divine life and love. Our prayer, in this portion of the Lord's Prayer, is a petition for the grace to release ourselves totally to the transformation which the Spirit wishes to effect in us, so that through us his kingdom may come to others.

28 *"Your will be done on earth as it is in heaven."* (Mt 6:10)

Jesus' first wish was always to do the will of his Father. Many times he reminded us of this. For Jesus, the will of the Father was not some sort of blind obedience but rather a gift of himself to the Father in love. When we love someone, we make every effort to please that person. Loving God means doing what pleases him. The Father's will is our salvation.

29 *"Give us today our daily bread."* (Mt 6:11)

We turn with confidence and trust to our provident Father, begging him to supply graciously all our needs each day. This petition brings us to a deeper awareness of our total dependence upon God, our Father. It also enkindles in us a more fervent spirit of gratitude for all his boundless gifts and blessings daily showered upon us.

30 *"And forgive us the wrong we have done as we forgive those who wrong us."*

(Mt 6:12)

In seeking mercy and forgiveness we turn to Jesus, our Savior and Redeemer. Jesus is now in his glory at the right hand of the Father, but his glory is to continue his redemptive work among us. He is pleased when we recognize our need for him as Savior and Redeemer.

31 *"Subject us not to the trial but deliver us from the evil one."* (Mt 6:13)

We attribute the work of sanctification in the world to the Holy Spirit. Today let us ask him to give us the wisdom and understanding to be able to recognize and discern any danger or evil threatening our spiritual growth. Let us also pray that the Holy Spirit will give us the courage, strength, and fortitude to conquer every allurement and temptation of the evil one.

Lord, Teach Us to Pray

JESUS ENCOURAGES AND URGES US to be faithful in developing a prayer life. Paul takes up the same refrain when he advises us to pray constantly, to pray perseveringly. Augustine tells us that praying without ceasing means to desire continually the eternal happiness of heaven. The more frequently we ask, the more intense will be our desire, the richer will be our prayer life.

Next we turn to the prayer of listening. Listening is loving. Listening is praying. We need to build into the structure of our lives a time each morning or evening to be still, to relax, to be silent, to listen, to be with the Lord.

If we understand prayer solely as a dialog with the Lord, it usually ends up as a monolog. The essence of prayer is union with God, not dialog. Union is established by listening.

After this follows a number of scriptural

passages reminding us that Jesus is present in his word. In prayer we meet him in his word in order to let him be present to us, and we, in turn, are present to him. His word is his personal and private communication with us. As we pray with his word, we can say with the psalmist: "A lamp to my feet is your word, / a light to my path" (Ps 119:105).

Jesus was a peripatetic teacher. He taught wherever and whenever people gathered to hear him. In his divine wisdom he used metaphors, examples, and images to explain profound truths or to teach moral principles. The parable of the sower (Lk 8:4-15) is a striking pastoral image outlining the dispositions so essential to permit his word to find a home in our heart and there to mold and transform us. The scriptural passages suggested toward the close of the month focus on the parable of the sower.

1 *One day he was praying in a certain place. When he had finished, one of his disciples asked him, "Lord, teach us to pray." (Lk 11:1)*

There are two gifts involved in prayer. Our gift is the ascetical part of prayer. We must give the Lord time, relax in his presence, be attentive to his inspirations, and listen to his word. The second gift comes from the Lord. The inspirations, insights, experiences of his loving presence, along with the peace and joy we feel are all God's gift to us.

Lord, teach us how to enter into a deep, personal union with you in prayer.

2 *When he had sent them away, he went up on the mountain by himself to pray. (Mt 14:23)*

Jesus not only taught us the importance and necessity for time spent in prayer, but he also showed us some of the hurdles we would have to overcome. At times we, too, must leave the crowd to be alone with Jesus. We have to set aside all the annoyances and arrange time for prayer as Jesus did. If Jesus needed time for prayer, how much more do we?

3 *Rejoice in hope, be patient under trial, persevere in prayer.* (Rom 12:12)

Prayer is the secret to our spiritual growth and development. If we are faithful in prayer, we will never lose hope even though dark clouds seem to threaten us. On the contrary, hope will be the source of our joy. Likewise when trial and difficulties arise, the time spent in prayer will help us see God's divine design which will keep us "patient under trial."

4 *"Ask, and you will receive. Seek, and you will find. Knock, and it will be opened to you. For the one who asks, receives. The one who seeks, finds. The one who knocks, enters."* (Mt 7:7-8)

The prayer of petition is an important method of praying. When we petition God, we are recognizing our own inadequacy. We are acknowledging our total dependence upon him. Repeated asking helps us to clarify the petitions in our own minds and increases our desire for whatever we are seeking from our loving Father.

5 *"This is my beloved Son on whom my favor rests. Listen to him."* (Mt 17:5)

The prayer of listening is a deep, fruitful, transforming method of praying. The Father instructs us to listen to Jesus, not merely to his words, but to contemplate his attitudes and action. Listening with our whole being will help us form the image of Jesus within ourselves.

6 *Rejoice always, never cease praying, render constant thanks; such is God's will for you in Christ Jesus.* (1 Thes 5:16-18)

There are three distinct marks which identify a Christian. A Christian is a happy person, exuding joy as he or she walks in the light of God's love. A Christian is a praying person, keeping in touch with the Lord. A Christian is always a grateful person. Regardless of how bleak the day may seem, there are blessings to count. If we face the sun, the shadows will fall behind us, but if we turn our back to the sun, the shadows are in front of us.

7 *At every opportunity pray in the Spirit, using prayers of every sort. Pray constantly and attentively for all in the holy company.*

(Eph 6:18)

We are praying "in the Spirit" when we give ourselves totally to the Holy Spirit so that he may release the floodgates of his love upon us. The Holy Spirit wants to envelop our human spirit with his divine Spirit. In this way he not only prays in us, but also fills us with his special fruits— love, peace, and joy (Gal 5:22).

8 *"Be on guard, and pray that you may not undergo the test."* (Mt 26:41)

When Jesus faced the terrible trial in the garden of Gethsemane, he used the occasion to beg us to pray that no temptation or trial, no conflict or cross, no disappointment or discouragement would be too great for us. Prayer is the source from which we derive the wisdom, courage, and strength to face the happenings of every day. As the poet says: "More things are wrought by prayer than this world dreams of."

9 *Pray perseveringly, be attentive in prayer, and pray in a spirit of thanksgiving.* (Col 4:2)

Paul gives us three important dispositions for prayer. Since prayer is our personal visit with the God of heaven and earth, we must be attentive to him who wants us to enjoy this faith experience.

Just as we eat regularly to maintain our physical well-being, so we must eat consistently at the table of the Lord's word to grow and mature in our following of Jesus. Then our hearts will overflow with gratitude, and we will be praying "in the spirit of thanksgiving."

10 *"Speak, Lord, for your servant is listening."* (1 Sm 3:9)

This prayer of Samuel enables us to form an ideal prayer posture. Like Samuel, we listen expectantly to what the Lord will ask of us. Like Mary, we sit quietly, calmly, attentively at the feet of Jesus listening intently to what he wishes to speak to our hearts. A given period each day in this kind of prayer will transform our whole mind and heart according to the heart of Jesus. Jesus said, "Learn from me, for I am gentle and humble of heart" (Mt 11:29).

11 *"Come to me heedfully, / listen, that you may have life."* (Is 55:3)

Listening is loving. Listening to the Lord is praying. When we listen to the Lord and give him our full attention, we are making the gift of ourselves to him that he may guide and inspire us, that he may encourage and strengthen us. When we listen to the Lord, we are permitting him to love us. Quiet, attentive listening is not only the first requisite for prayer, but it is prayer.

12 *Wait for the Lord and keep his way.*
(Ps 37:34)

Waiting is an ideal prayer posture. We are to wait *on* the Lord just as a waiter waits on us when we eat in a public dining room. Waiting means being attentive to the movements of his Spirit within us. It means being for the Lord and letting him be for us. When we "keep his way," we are waiting on the Lord.

13 *Wait for the Lord with courage; / be stout-hearted, and wait for the Lord.* (Ps 27:14)

Times of trial and stress help us to recognize our own poverty, our own inadequacy. When we acknowledge our total dependence on the Lord, we are being prepared to listen more attentively to him. If we listen prayerfully, we will recall the caring, concerned love which the Lord has always shown us. Listening patiently and trustingly will help us "wait for the Lord with courage."

14 *"Listen to what I say: / Open your eyes and see! / The fields are shining for harvest!"* (Jn 4:35)

Listening is putting ourselves, as much as we can, into a position to see and feel what the other person is experiencing. Jesus sees the countless souls without a shepherd, unable to hear and recognize his voice. He is calling us to minister to them, by first listening to his plan and program and then by entering the harvest field with zeal and enthusiasm. Our listening daily will show us the way.

15 *"This is my Son, my Chosen One. Listen to him."* (Lk 9:35)

Listening at the core of our being means giving ourselves totally to the Lord. When we listen, we strive to set aside the pre-occupations of the moment. We strive to empty our minds and hearts in order to be completely available to the Lord. This attentive listening is the gift of ourselves. This is the gift Jesus wants. He is not so much concerned about what we are trying to accomplish for him, but rather what we are. This kind of listening is a gift. It is prayer.

16 *"Listen carefully to this."* (Mk 4:3)

The word of God has a power to cleanse, mold, and transform our whole heart. However, to be effective we must be willing to listen to God's word. We must let it find a home in our heart. A man could starve to death with a table of luscious food before him if he refused to eat. God is eager to nourish and nurture us with his word if we are willing to listen. We must be receptive.

17 *"Let everyone heed what he hears!"* (Mt 13:9)

The Lord is present in his word. He invites us to listen to his word. He speaks his word to us through the inspirations and insights which come to us. His word may even nudge us with the little hunches which motivate us throughout the day. If we listen prayerfully and regularly, even daily, his word becomes loud and clear, bringing us great peace and joy.

18 *In the beginning was the Word; / the Word was in God's presence, / and the Word was God.* (Jn 1:1)

Jesus is the reverberation of the Father. Jesus is present in his word. In fact, he is the Word of God. Vatican Council II reminded us that "He [Jesus] is present in His word, since it is He Himself who speaks when the holy scriptures are read in the Church."

It behooves us to listen attentively to him speaking to us.

19 *Humbly welcome the word that has taken root in you, with its power to save you. Act on this word. If all you do is listen to it, you are deceiving yourselves.* (Jas 1:21-22)

God's word has the power to save because it can transform us completely. As we ponder his word, it will mold our thoughts to be more and more in conformity with the mind of Jesus. It can effect a conversion within us without us even recognizing it. The only condition required is for us to "humbly welcome the word that has taken root in us."

20 *Let the word of Christ, rich as it is, dwell in you.* (Col 3:16)

When seed is planted in the loose soil of a garden, it remains dormant until it is watered by a gentle rain. Then it begins to germinate and grow. The warm rays of the sun stimulate its growth and bring it to fruition. If we give the plant tender care, it will produce abundantly.

Our hearts are gardens in which the word is planted. We are the gardeners. Our response to his word will determine the fruitfulness.

21 *"So shall my word be / that goes forth from my mouth. / It shall not return to me void, / but shall do my will, / achieving the end for which I sent it."* (Is 55:11)

Our provident Father sends the snow and rain to water the earth and make it fertile and fruitful. In our spiritual growth he sends his word to nurture, enlighten, encourage, and strengthen us to produce a rich harvest in our own lives. His word will be operative in energizing us to the extent that we are cooperative.

22 *"You are clean already, / thanks to the word I have spoken to you."* (Jn 15:3)

The word of the Lord has a powerful transforming energy. Jesus told the apostles that when they listened to him, they were not only made clean, but were being molded and transformed. If we sit at the feet of Jesus in prayer, his word will transform our hearts, making them more and more like his heart. We will become more like him, since we become what we contemplate.

Lord Jesus, hasten that day!

23 *Indeed, God's word is living and effective, sharper than any two-edged sword.*

(Heb 4:12)

The word of God is incisive. As we ponder his word, we will more easily recognize our own shortcomings and rationalizations. We will, also, see more clearly if our dispositions and lifestyles are in conformity with his word. The incisiveness of that two-edged sword will help us rid ourselves of what is not of the Lord and effect a conversion process in our hearts if we permit it.

24 *"The word is near you, on your lips, and in your heart." . . . For if you confess with your lips that Jesus is Lord, and believe in your heart that God raised him from the dead, you will be saved.* (Rom 10:8-9)

If we sincerely and wholeheartedly believe that Jesus is Lord, then his word will produce in our hearts a dynamic, operative faith committing us to proclaim the good news, not only with our lips, but by our lifestyle also. This kind of faith in action will assure us of our eternal salvation, and we will not come alone. Many will follow in our footsteps.

Parable of the Sower

*A farmer went out to sow some seed. In the
sowing, some fell on the footpath where it was
walked on and the birds of the air ate it up.
Some fell on rocky ground, sprouted up, then
withered through lack of moisture. Some fell
among briers, and the thorns growing up with
it stifled it. But some fell on good soil, grew up,
and yielded grain a hundredfold. . . .*

*This is the meaning of the parable. The seed
is the word of God. Those on the footpath are
people who hear, but the devil comes and takes
the word out of their hearts lest they believe
and be saved. Those on the rocky ground are
the ones who, when they hear the word, receive
it with joy. They have no root; they believe for
a while, but fall away in time of temptation.
The seed fallen among briers are those who
hear, but their progress is stifled by the cares
and riches and pleasures of life and they do not
mature. The seed on good ground are those
who hear the word in a spirit of openness,
retain it, and bear fruit through perseverance.*
(Lk 8:5-15)

25 *"A farmer went out to sow some seed."*
(Lk 8:5)

It is within the realm of possibility that the large crowd which gathered to hear Jesus was at the same time observing a farmer on a hillside sowing his seed. The terrain was very rocky allowing only little thatches of grain to be sown among the rocks.

As we picture this field in our imagination and listen to the parable of Jesus, we will begin to look at ourselves to determine how well we might be receiving the word of God.

26 *"The seed is the word of God."* (Lk 8:11)

This brief statement contains a wealth of implications. In the first place, the God of might and majesty, the Lord of heaven and earth, wants to communicate with us privately. Doesn't that stagger the imagination! Second, Jesus is present in his word living in our hearts. He is operative and dynamic in us, empowering his word to transform us. How precious is that seed! How intently we ought to listen to every nuance of his word.

27 *"Let everyone who has ears attend to what he has heard."* (Lk 8:8)

Jesus came to bring us the good news of God's enduring love for us personally and individually. He revealed the good news of our redemption and salvation. His word is the beacon directing us through the maze of conflicting ideologies that wean us away from the pathway leading to our eternal destiny. His word is his love.

28 *"In the sowing, some fell on the footpath where it was walked on and the birds of the air ate it up."* (Lk 8:5)

Jesus himself explained the meaning of the seed which fell on the pathway. "Those on the footpath are people who hear, but the devil comes and takes the word out of their hearts lest they believe and be saved."

Perhaps an inspiration or an insight came to us encouraging us to reach out in love to someone. Perhaps we might have excused ourselves for not responding to it. We can easily rationalize ourselves in or out of something without even being aware of it.

29 *"Some fell on rocky ground, sprouted up, then withered through lack of moisture."* (Lk 8:6)

Again Jesus explained the meaning of the seed on rocky ground. "Those on rocky ground are the ones who, when they hear the word, receive it with joy. They have no root; they believe for awhile, but fall away in time of temptation."

As we reflect on our own lives, we will, no doubt, discover occasions when our enthusiasm withered away, or certain obstacles and difficulties seemed insurmountable; hence we gave up.

30 *"Some fell among briers, and the thorns growing up with it stifled it."* (Lk 8:7)

Jesus did not want us to miss the point, so he explained: "The seed fallen among briers are those who hear, but their progress is stifled by the cares and riches and pleasures of life and they do not mature." We have paved many roads with our good intentions, but the magnetic power of less important things often takes priority in our lives. A little reflection will give us a good assessment of our lifestyle.

31 *"But some fell on good soil, grew up, and yielded grain a hundredfold."* (Lk 8:8)

A noted spiritual writer said that if we think we are in any of the first categories—footpath, rocky ground—we should rejoice and relax, because we are probably on the good soil.

If we continue to bask in the light of God's presence and if we keep our soil porous by being receptive to the gentle rain of God's grace, our harvest will be an abundant yield.

Called to Serve

W^{E ARE A PRIVILEGED PEOPLE.} We have been personally invited by Jesus to follow him and become his disciples. A disciple is a person who follows the master so closely that he can be identified with the master. We are called to "put on that new man created in God's image" (Eph 4:24). This is our unique prerogative and privilege.

During the first part of the month we will listen to Jesus calling us personally and individually into discipleship. In the scriptural passages suggested we also hear Jesus telling us what is expected of us as his disciples. May our response be as gracious and eager as was Isaiah's: "Here I am, send me!" (Is 6:8).

Then in days 18 to 24, Paul describes the attitudes of Jesus in responding to his ministry (Phil 2:5-11). The verses of this hymn extol the attitudes of Jesus and the way of life he lived to complete his mission. As disciples we find hope and encouragement in the words of this hymn. Woven throughout is a challenge to us. Jesus shows us the way: "Jesus Christ was not alternately yes and no; he was never anything but yes" (2 Cor 1:19).

From day 25 to 31 we listen to Jesus' own words outlining a pattern for our imitation. His words may cause us some concern or even frighten us momentarily, until we recall the privilege of being a disciple and the reward which accompanies our following Jesus.

Jesus loves us with a boundless love. That fathomless love helped him shoulder his cross and carry it on to victory. "The burden of love is light like a cloud," says a Bantu proverb. Our love for him will likewise make "our yoke easy and our burden light."

1 *"Come and see."* (Jn 1:39)

Jesus' invitation to "come and see" is consistent throughout the first part of the gospel. Jesus always invited prospective disciples to "come and see" who he was and what his ministry was all about.

That same invitation reaches down through the ages until it reaches our own ears. Jesus is inviting us to "come and see" who it is before we make our commitment to follow him. Jesus never tried to deceive or trick anyone into becoming his disciple.

In the quiet time we spend with him, he will reveal more about himself and our role in his kingdom.

2 *"Come, see for yourself."* (Jn 1:46)

We can learn very much about Jesus intellectually and theologically, but we really need to know him with our heart in order to know him as a personal God who loves us just as we are.

In silence and solitude, in the depth of our own heart, we discover that he is our gracious, loving Lord who lives with us every moment of our journey through life. We need to spend time with him regularly in order to form a deeper friendship with him. That is prayer at its best.

3 *"Follow me." Matthew got up and followed him. (Mt 9:9)*

As members of the Body of Christ we are never alone going down the solitary trail of life. Others have trodden the same path before us showing us the way by their example.

Matthew is our brother-disciple who left his post as a tax collector to follow Jesus. In moments of hesitation or fear, or when doubting our own ability to live out our commitment, we can be assured that Matthew and the whole heavenly host are interceding for us as they accompany us every step of the way.

4 *"Your business is to follow me." (Jn 21:22)*

Like Peter, we can easily become unduly concerned about those around us and about the role they are to fulfill in life. When we become so engrossed in the happenings around us, we can readily lose our focus on the Lord. It is then that Jesus may address the same words to us: "Your business is to follow me."

If we keep our eyes riveted on Jesus, we will become more like him. We will be reflecting his presence to others. This is our apostolate.

5 *"This is how all will know you for my disciples; / your love for one another."*

(Jn 13:35)

We communicate effectively by means of the vibrations which reach those around us. Our actions and attitudes also speak eloquently. Jesus stated it: "By their fruits you will know them."

Jesus assured us that our love for one another will certainly label us as his disciples more effectively than mere words. As his disciples, we are called to be lovingly concerned about all our brothers and sisters.

6 *"My Father has been glorified / in your bearing much fruit / and becoming my disciples."* (Jn 15:8)

In this allegory, Jesus says: "I am the vine, you are the branches." It is the branch which blossoms and bears the fruit, yet the branch cannot exist without the vine. Jesus permits us to bear the fruit even though apart from him "we can do nothing." Realizing such boundless goodness, we will give glory to the Father. To this we are called as disciples of the Lord.

7 *"If you seek perfection, go, sell your posses- sions, and give to the poor. You will then have treasure in heaven. Afterward, come back and follow me."* (Mt 19:21)

Jesus is speaking here of an inordinate attachment to temporalities. We cannot serve two masters. In the hierarchy of priorities there can be only one number one. The Lord must be that number one, then all the pieces of the jigsaw puzzle of life begin to fit together. Furthermore, detachment from mundane preoccupa- tions gives us a newfound freedom and a reward which bears fruit in eternity.

Today pray Psalm 1 attentively and fervently.

8 *"I will be your follower wherever you go."* *Jesus said to him, "The foxes have lairs, the birds of the sky have nests, but the Son of Man has nowhere to lay his head."* (Lk 9:57-58)

Jesus made it perfectly clear that he was offering no great earthly reward except the peace and joy which come from loving and serving him. His words are our challenge.

Winston Churchill paraphrased the words of Jesus at the outbreak of World War II when he told his nation: "All I have to offer you is blood, sweat, and tears." His people rallied to that challenge.

Daily the dedicated disciple of Jesus rallies to his call of radical discipleship.

9 *"Come after me." The man replied, "Let me bury my father first." Jesus said to him, "Let the dead bury their dead; come away and proclaim the kingdom of God." (Lk 9:59-60)*

At first glance the words of Jesus may seem harsh, unfeeling, and impersonal, until we understand just what the man was saying. He wanted to become a disciple of Jesus only after his whole family died and he had no one else left in this world.

Jesus put our desires into the proper focus when he said: "Seek first his kingship over you, his way of holiness, and all these things will be given you besides" (Mt 6:33).

10 *"I will be your follower, Lord, but first let me take leave of my people at home." Jesus answered him, "Whoever puts his hand to the plow but keeps looking back is unfit for the reign of God." (Lk 9:61)*

A farmer cannot plow a straight furrow if he keeps looking back. Likewise, no one can be a true disciple if he or she makes only a half-hearted commitment or keeps looking in two directions. Furthermore if a person's commitment is not a total commitment, his or her ministry will become routine, difficult, if not outright drudgery.

11 *"My sheep hear my voice. / I know them, / and they follow me."* (Jn 10:27)

If we are faithful followers of Jesus, like sheep attentive to their shepherd, our minds and hearts will be in tune with that of the Good Shepherd. We will hear his voice as he guides, encourages, and energizes us through the inspiration, enlightenment, and strength he sends our way.

Just as a radio or television is a proper receiver to transmit sound and pictures for our enjoyment, so our hearts and minds are the receivers to bring the Good Shepherd's voice to us. We must stay tuned in.

12 *Jesus raised his eyes to heaven, pronounced a blessing, broke the loaves, and gave them to the disciples to distribute.* (Mk 6:41)

When Jesus multiplied the loaves and fish to feed the multitude, he could have also distributed them by his own divine power. Instead, he gave them to the disciples to distribute.

Jesus does the same with us. He calls upon us to proclaim the good news, to make him known, to radiate his love by reflecting the peace and joy with which he fills us. "Jesus has no hands, but our hands, no feet, but our feet, no voice but our voice."

13 *"If anyone would serve me, / let him follow me; / where I am, / there will my servant be."* (Jn 12:26)

A disciple does not merely listen to the teaching of the master, but he follows him diligently listening to his words, observing his attitudes toward others, striving to absorb the mind and heart of the master.

Jesus wants us to keep ourselves aware of his abiding presence with us, listening to the promptings of his grace, being attentive to his inspirations. We condition ourselves for this attitude of mind and heart by meeting Jesus daily in prayer. Then we will not only be following in his footsteps, but we will be identified with Jesus.

14 *"Come after me and I will make you fishers of men."* (Mt 4:19)

Jesus calls us to be his followers that we may know him as our personal, loving God. He fills us with his love, peace, and joy that we may become channels through which he reaches out to others.

Wittingly or unwittingly we fulfill this mission in life by all we say and do, our actions, our attitudes and dispositions. As followers of Jesus, we are always "front and center." Thus we draw others into the circle of his special friends.

15 *"What I just did was to give you an example: / as I have done, so you must do."*
(Jn 13:15)

Jesus lived to the full everything he taught. He invites us, as his disciples, to come and see how he lived, how he prayed, and what he taught.

The only way we can successfully teach a spiritual truth or a way of life is by our own example. We must live what we teach. Our own way of life must be in conformity with the principles we propose to others. This is the real badge of discipleship.

16 *"Unless the grain of wheat falls to the earth and dies, / it remains just a grain of wheat. / But if it dies, / it produces much fruit."*
(Jn 12:24)

This pastoral image is a perfect illustration of a truism which confronts us often in daily life. We shun suffering, restraint, sacrifice. We need to die to self, to empty ourselves so that the Lord can fill us with himself and with his transforming power and love. This dying to self "produces much fruit."

17 *"Go, therefore, and make disciples of all the nations." (Mt 28:19)*

In the beginning of his public life, Jesus invited his followers to come to him, to listen to the good news of salvation, to learn his way of life. It was only toward the end of his life that he commissioned them to "go" and proclaim the gospel message.

Jesus, likewise, invites us to come to him daily to let him mold and transform us, then he commissions us to go and proclaim his way of life in word and deed. We are reminded of that commission at each Mass: "Go in peace to love and serve the Lord."

18 *Your attitude must be that of Christ. (Phil 2:5)*

This verse introduces a praise-filled hymn which reflects the humility, the self-effacement, the obedience of Jesus. These verses portray Jesus as the ideal model of Christian service.

Paul points out these virtues of Jesus with the hope that we will follow in his footprints. A follower of Jesus must always be more concerned about others than about self—not only his or her own glory, but the glory of God. This was Jesus' attitude. May it be ours!

19 *Though he was in the form of God, / he did not deem equality with God / something to be grasped at.* (Phil 2:6)

The "form of God" was Jesus' divine nature. He did not give up his divinity when he took on our human nature. It always remained his essence.

Though a baby, a child, a youth, and an adult all retain the essence of a person, exterior changes do take place with the passing of years.

Retaining his divine nature, Jesus took on our human nature in order to redeem our sinful nature, thus endowing us with his divine life and making us temples of the Holy Spirit.

20 *Rather, he emptied himself / and took the form of a slave, / being born in the likeness of men.* (Phil 2:7)

Jesus emptied himself of his divinity to take upon himself our humanity. This was not some form of play acting, but a reality. He was truly man. The two natures in Jesus will forever remain a mystery. It is useless to ask how; we can only stand in awe and reverence of him who is almighty God and yet also hungry, weary, and in tears.

Only divine love can explain why!

21 *He was known to be of human estate, / and it was thus that he humbled himself, / obediently accepting even death, / death on a cross!* (Phil 2:8)

"Death on a cross" was the most painful and the most shameful type of execution known in that day. Jesus obediently accepted death because he came to do the will of the Father and not his own. He came not to exalt himself, but to renounce his glory for our sake.

If humility, obedience, and self-renunciation were the characteristics of the life of Jesus, they must be the hallmarks of our life and the life of every Christian. Selfishness and pride destroy our likeness to Jesus and our love for one another.

22 *Because of this, / God highly exalted him / and bestowed on him the name / above every other name.* (Phil 2:9)

Jesus' self-renunciation brought him greater glory. Jesus himself repeatedly taught that everyone who humbles himself will be exalted (Mt 23:12; Lk 14:11). Surely there could never be a more humbling experience than Jesus willingly accepted. How rightly he deserves to be exalted and loved! How holy and sacred is his name!

23 *So that at Jesus' name, / every knee must bend / in the heavens, on the earth, / and under the earth.* (Phil 2:10)

Jesus' willing sacrifice on the cross paved the way for every creature "in the heavens, on the earth and under the earth" to worship, adore, reverence and above all to love him. When we ponder the thought that Jesus renounced his glory and died on the cross for us, we cannot possibly resist such love, nor refuse to respond to it.

24 *And every tongue proclaim / to the glory of God the Father: / JESUS CHRIST IS LORD!* (Phil 2:11)

These four words were the first creed found in the early Christian church. It is a very simple creed, but it is all-embracing. The plan and desire of God is that all creation proclaim that "JESUS CHRIST IS LORD."

Jesus becomes the Lord of our life when we accept the gospel way of life as he taught it. When we recognize that he has called us to follow him as dedicated and devoted disciples, when we listen and respond to his will, then he is truly Lord of our life.

Discipleship

Jesus said to all: "Whoever wishes to be my follower must deny his very self, take up his cross each day, and follow in my steps. Whoever would save his life will lose it, and whoever loses his life for my sake will save it. What profit does he show who gains the whole world and destroys himself in the process? If a man is ashamed of me and my doctrine, the Son of Man will be ashamed of him when he comes in his glory and that of his Father and his holy angels." (Lk 9:23-26)

25 *Jesus said to all: "Whoever wishes to be my follower must deny his very self, take up his cross each day, and follow in my steps."*

(Lk 9:23)

As children we played a game called follow the leader. The leader would attempt daring and difficult feats, such as jumping over an object, or scaling a low wall. Thus he challenged his followers to do the same.

Jesus is our leader. He not only challenges us to follow him, but he goes with us to support and encourage us. His game is real. If, with his grace, we do succeed in overcoming every obstacle, our reward is one without compare—eternal happiness with him.

26 *"Whoever wishes to be my follower must deny his very self, take up his cross each day, and follow in my steps."* (Lk 9:23)

Jesus invites us to become his followers, but he does not trick anyone into becoming his disciple. He spells out the conditions very plainly. Since our human nature resists difficulties and hardships, we are apt to think of the price of discipleship, rather than the privilege of being invited to be in the company of Jesus. When we reflect that the invitation is from Jesus himself, then the price seems right, the privilege tremendous, and the reward without equal.

27 *"Whoever wishes to be my follower must deny his very self, take up his cross each day, and follow in my steps."* (Lk 9:23)

To deny ourselves means a dying to self. This seems absolutely incongruous to anyone in pursuit of happiness in this world. However, there is a paradox here. We die to self many times a day without realizing it. When we keep an appointment, speak a kind word, open a door, or perform a duty, we are dying to self. We discover that there is more joy in giving than in receiving. In his divine wisdom Jesus knew that dying to self would bring us genuine happiness, peace, and fulfillment.

28 *"Whoever wishes to be my follower must deny his very self, take up his cross each day, and follow in my steps."* (Lk 9:23)

When our will runs parallel with God's will, like two railroad tracks, we encounter no crosses. However, when our will runs perpendicular to God's will, we will encounter a heavy cross. We have a tendency to think of a cross as something negative, painful, disagreeable. At times that may well be, until we realize that every cross is a stepping stone to closer union with God.

29 *"Whoever wishes to be my follower must deny his very self, take up his cross each day, and follow in my steps."* (Lk 9:23)

Jesus never asks us to break new ground in following him. He leads the way and bids us to follow in his footsteps. At times our following may be easy, like walking leisurely down a smooth trail. At other times it may be steep and rugged.

Picture a small child trying to walk in his father's footprints in the snow. The father's lengthier stride challenges the child's strength to the full. In following Jesus, we can be certain that he waits for us along the trail if we tire. He will even retrace his steps to rescue us if we fall or need his help.

30 *"Whoever would save his life will lose it, and whoever loses his life for my sake will save it."* (Lk 9:24)

Obviously Jesus is contrasting our temporal life and our eternal life. If our sole ambition is to amass a fortune, whether by just or unjust means, to revel in all sorts of self-indulgence, then our eternal salvation is endangered. On the other hand, to totally neglect our temporal well-being and that of our family is also wrong. Virtue stands in the middle course with the proper focus on both.

31 *"What profit does he show who gains the whole world and destroys himself in the process?"* (Lk 9:25)

With our fallen human nature and our brokenness, pride, power, and riches can become such an obsession that we ruin our health in the process. Our materialistic world judges success only by the size of a bank account. We can easily be imbued with these secularistic standards.

A virtuous life gives a proper balance in our daily striving. If our focus is always on the Lord and his will, we can be assured of genuine happiness.

Jesus Programs a Lifestyle

J ESUS CAME INTO THIS WORLD as a teacher. Even his enemies addressed him as teacher. Jesus himself accepted the title and office of teacher when he said: "You address me as 'Teacher' and 'Lord' / and fittingly enough, / for that is what I am" (Jn 13:13).

Without question Jesus was a teacher par excellence. Jesus knew well that a spiritual truth or a moral principle could not be taught merely by words, but that the master must witness by his own way of life to all that he teaches. Jesus lived out in his own life everything he asks us to believe and put into practice in our lives. Even more, he abides with us to aid and assist us to live daily in conformity with his way of life.

We begin our daily prayer this month with some of the maxims which Jesus presented in the Sermon on the Mount (Lk 6:27ff). These maxims offer some guidelines and directives for our journeying through life.

As we continue our prayer for this month, we find that Jesus insisted upon two all-important dispositions which every Christian should manifest—joy and humility. A joyous person is a humble person, and a humble person is also a joyful person. A number of scriptural passages are suggested which should help us cultivate these desirable dispositions.

Toward the end of the month we will pray with a set of principles which Jesus taught called the Beatitudes. They are paradoxical, to say the least. The values which Jesus proposed are opposed to conventional values. Jesus pronounces a blessing on those who do not share in the conventional values of the world, but who strive to live up to the standards which he set forth. The moral revolution which the Beatitudes should effect has not yet been achieved in all its fullness, but the followers of Jesus, who set the Beatitudes as their goal in life, experience much peace and joy as they look forward to the promise of eternal happiness in heaven.

1 *"Do to others what you would have them do to you."* (Lk 6:31)

This ancient maxim was always stated in the negative: "Avoid doing to others what you yourself would not want done to you." Jesus stated it in the positive to implement his teaching on the love of neighbor. Do not just *avoid* doing harm to a neighbor, but rather *seek* ways and means of doing good for another person. Furthermore, do not wait to be asked for help, but reach out in love on your own initiative.

2 *"Be compassionate, as your Father is compassionate."* (Lk 6:36)

The Father is infinite compassion because he is infinite love. In spite of our sinfulness, our self-centeredness, our half-hearted response to his magnanimous love, the Father continues to love us anyway. He loves us just as we are, regardless of what we have done.

This is a real challenge for our daily living—to love others regardless of who they are, regardless of what they have said or done. Such a Christlike attitude will lead many to the Lord.

3 *"Give and it shall be given to you. Good measure pressed down, shaken together, running over, will they pour into the fold of your garment."* (Lk 6:38)

When we think of giving, we immediately think about offering a monetary gift. There is much more to giving as Jesus did. Sometimes it means giving our time to a person who needs to be heard, using our gifts and talents to assist someone, or being available to a family member or friend who needs to know that they are loved and appreciated. We are also giving when we are sincere with our compliments and gratitude. Giving includes accepting a gift from someone who also has the need to give. Jesus included all of this and more.

4 *"A good tree does not produce decayed fruit any more than a decayed tree produces good fruit. Each tree is known by its yield."* (Lk 6:43-44)

We, too, are known by our fruits. We may speak of living a deeply committed Christian life, when our own life is not in conformity with what we say. The only way to teach a spiritual truth, is by witnessing. Some people may be eloquent and learned in proclaiming the gospel message, but their actions and attitudes may not give witness to their message. This will render their message totally ineffective.

5 *"Love your enemies, do good to those who hate you; bless those who curse you and pray for those who maltreat you."* (Lk 6:27-28)

This directive from the lips of Jesus is diametrically opposed to what the world would advocate. This mandate seems more attainable when we discover why we have so-called enemies. Usually they are people who are hurting deep within themselves. They may be angry, jealous, insecure, resentful, rejected. They need to ventilate their feelings on someone, and we happen to be their victim. This may even be an indication of the love and respect they have for us. We need to remember the prayer of Jesus: "Father, forgive them; they do not know what they are doing" (Lk 23:34).

6 *"Pardon, and you shall be pardoned."*
(Lk 6:37)

"Forgive and forget" is an oft-repeated adage, but to put this wholesome advice into practice is far more difficult. The brief prayer, "Lord, heal me," repeated many times throughout the day will bring much grace and healing. God accepts our intentions and our desire to forgive and forget even if we cannot seemingly forgive and forget totally. If we are trying honestly and sincerely, the Lord is pleased.

7 *"Do not judge, and you will not be judged. Do not condemn, and you will not be condemned."* (Lk 6:37)

When we pass judgment on another person, we are, in reality, manifesting our own weaknesses and our own problem areas. Otherwise, we would not notice them in someone else. Also, we are looking merely at the exterior, rather than at the heart. No human being can know the heart of another. We are the sum-total of our life's experiences and the impressions they left upon us. That area is known to God alone.

8 *"You have nothing to fear! I come to proclaim good news to you—tidings of great joy to be shared by the whole people."* (Lk 2:10)

The era of redemption was announced by the angels to the shepherds at Bethlehem as a time of great joy. Christmas is still a time of great joy, since it recalls for us that "God so loved the world that he gave his only Son" (Jn 3:16). We can celebrate Christmas each day, since Jesus is born eucharistically on our altars at Mass. This truth is a tremendous source of joy!

9 *"My being proclaims the greatness of the Lord, / my spirit finds joy in God my savior."*
(Lk 1:46-47)

Mary must have been ecstatic when she realized that the long-awaited Redeemer was to come. How humbled she must have been to have been chosen by God as the instrument through which the Savior was to come!

Mary rejoiced, too, because God was faithful to his promise: "My love shall never leave you / nor my covenant of peace be shaken" (Is 54:10).

10 *"I tell you truly: / you will weep and mourn / while the world rejoices; / you will grieve for a time, / but your grief will be turned into joy."*
(Jn 16:20)

Jesus had to tread the painful way of the cross before we could experience the joys of the resurrection. Our own way of the cross may seem terribly agonizing at times, but it will eventually culminate in the ecstatic joy of an eternal resurrection.

There can be no crown without a cross. Keeping our vision on the heavenly horizon will alleviate much of the pain and lighten the burden as we walk down the pathway of life.

11 *"You are sad for a time, / but I shall see you again; / then your hearts will rejoice / with a joy no one can take from you."* (Jn 16:22)

Joy is not so much the absence of sorrow and sadness as it is an awareness of God's abiding presence with us at every moment. Sadness may overtake us in times of suffering and rejection. We may even indulge in self-pity. But if we turn our focus on Jesus, recalling his powerful presence, the clouds of sadness will be lifted, and we will experience the joy which no one can take from us.

12 *"Ask and you shall receive, / that your joy may be full."* (Jn 16:24)

When we confidently and trustingly ask the Father for what we need, we are acknowledging our dependence upon him. It is really our profession of faith in his caring, concerned love. As we do so, we experience great joy. Joy arises from the realization that God wants to be a generous, gracious Abba lovingly providing for us and all his children. As we pause to reflect on his goodness to us, our joy will be full.

13 *"I tell you, there will likewise be more joy in heaven over one repentant sinner than over ninety-nine righteous people who have no need to repent."* (Lk 15:7)

When we, as sinners, turn to the Lord with a humble contrite heart, we are making ourselves receptive to the influx of our Savior's forgiving, healing, redeeming love. Paul reassures us of this love: "You can depend on this as worthy of full acceptance: that Christ Jesus came into the world to save sinners" (1 Tm 1:15).

When we become convinced that the Lord loves us just as we are, regardless of what we may have done, then our joy knows no bounds. Then we also enjoy great peace. All heaven rejoices with us.

14 *"I tell you, there will be the same kind of joy before the angels of God over one repentant sinner."* (Lk 15:10)

The angels in heaven are jubilant every time a sinner recognizes Jesus in the role which he cherishes most, that of Savior and Redeemer. The angels rejoice and praise God for his compassionate love and merciful forgiveness.

As sinners, we rejoice when we experience his great compassion and interior peace when he wipes out our sins and reestablishes our relationship with him.

15 *"All this I tell you / that my joy may be yours / and your joy may be complete."*
(Jn 15:11)

There cannot possibly be any news greater than the good news which Jesus revealed to us of the Father's fathomless love for us and his own bountiful love for us. This love wrought our salvation. This is the source of our joy. How delighted Jesus was to bring us this word and thus make our joy complete. Can there be any greater joy than knowing that we are so loved and made so lovable!

16 *"Learn from me, for I am gentle and humble of heart."* (Mt 11:29)

Jesus is always our pacesetter. He leads the way in everything he asks of us. Humility stands out as one of his divine attributes. "He humbled himself, obediently accepting death, death on a cross" (Phil 2:8).

Paul admonishes us: "Think humbly of others as superior to yourselves, each of you looking to the other's interests rather than to his own" (Phil 2:3).

17 *"For everyone who exalts himself shall be humbled."* (Lk 14:11)

A proud person is an unhappy person, with very few friends. Arrogance irritates others, and people shun arrogant company. Proud people are unhappy, too, because they are never satisfied, never fulfilled. They want the best for themselves; and if they obtain some measure of acknowledgment they want even more. Eventually the proud will be humbled, which could either devastate them or cause a great conversion.

18 *"He who humbles himself shall be exalted."* (Lk 14:11)

An unholy kind of pride plagues most of us all the days of our life. We need to pause frequently to examine our motives and intentions in performing certain tasks.

A very gifted and talented artist was complimented many times for her work. Her response to the many compliments was a simple "Thank you" to the person and a quiet "Thank you, God" to herself.

The humble person has a special spot in the Lord's heart.

19 *"He who humbles himself shall be exalted."*
(Lk 14:11)

Genuine humility recognizes that all gifts and blessings come from God. We are happy to use all these gifts for God's honor and glory, come what may to us.

A famous author's writings were always very much in demand by many leading publications. However, when he sent in a manuscript, he always included a return envelope with postage so that, if rejected, it could be returned to him. He was truly a humble person in spite of his great talents.

20 *"For everyone who exalts himself shall be humbled while he who humbles himself shall be exalted."* (Lk 18:14)

Jesus used a powerful example of genuine humility when he told the parable of the Pharisee and the tax collector going up to the Temple to pray. The Pharisee used the occasion to inform an apparently uninformed God how good he was. On the other hand the tax collector humbly prayed: "O God be merciful to me, a sinner."

Jesus made a strong point: "Believe me, this man went home from the temple justified but the other did not."

21 *"When you are invited by someone to a wedding party, do not sit in the place of honor in case some greater dignitary has been invited."* (Lk 14:8)

Jesus used a simple illustration to teach an eternal truth. Using the seating arrangement at a wedding, Jesus teaches us an important lesson on pride. The arrogant person will vie for a place of honor, while a truly humble person will be satisfied with the lowest place. The proud person seeks the best, the highest, the most for personal glory. He maintains: "The best is not too good for me."

Does this give us pause to reflect?

22 *"What you should do when you have been invited is to go and sit in the lowest place, so that when your host approaches you he will say, 'My friend, come up higher.'"* (Lk 14:10)

Taking the lowest place at table, or elsewhere, is not always a sign of genuine humility. A false humility may motivate a person to do so. This is sometimes humility with a hook. False humility will sit in the lowest place with the hope that the host will insist that the person move up higher. Such a person hopes that the display of humility will impress others.

23 *Be humbled in the sight of the Lord and he will raise you on high.* (Jas 4:10)

Humility is the recognition of our total dependence upon God and our own inability to accomplish anything ourselves without his help. This mentality is pleasing to the Lord. When we come before the Lord with this attitude of heart, then God can accomplish great things through us. We will then be raised on high, and God will be glorified.

The Beatitudes

How blest are the poor in spirit: the reign of
God is theirs.
Blest too are the sorrowing; they shall be
consoled.
Blest are the lowly; they shall inherit the land.
Blest are they who hunger and thirst for
holiness;
    they shall have their fill.
Blest are they who show mercy; mercy shall be
theirs.
Blest are the single-hearted for they shall see
God.
Blest too are the peacemakers; they shall be
called sons of God.
Blest are those persecuted for holiness' sake;
    the reign of God is theirs.
Blest are you when they insult you and
persecute you and utter every kind of
slander against you because of me.
Be glad and rejoice, for your reward is great in
heaven;
    they persecuted the prophets before you in
    the very same way.
       (Mt 5:3-12)

24 *"How blest are the poor in spirit; the reign of God is theirs."* (Mt 5:3)

This beatitude reminds us of our creature-liness. It reminds us of our inability to accomplish anything of ourselves. We need God's help for everything we do. Our recognition of our own inadequacy and poverty brings us many blessings.

When we realize our complete depen-dence on God, our reliance on and attach-ment to material things will be greatly diminished. We become materially poor as well. Then we will be blessed.

25 *"Blest too are the sorrowing; they shall be consoled."* (Mt 5:4)

This virtue is especially necessary today since we have lost our sense of sin. Our rationalizations help us to explain our moral conduct as a psychological need. On the other hand, repentance was the first doctrine which John the Baptist and Jesus himself preached. Sorrowing means pri-marily a sincere compunction for our own wrongdoing and for the sinfulness of the world. It also includes a sense of our own unworthiness. This attitude brings the Lord's forgiveness and healing.

26 *"Blest are the lowly; they shall inherit the land."* (Mt 5:5)

Without humility there can be no such thing as love, since the very beginning of love is a sense of unworthiness. Lowliness shows us our need to love and be loved. Humility helps us to recognize our need for forgiveness and also our need to learn. Learning begins with humility. Quintilian, a great Roman teacher, once said about his scholars: "They would no doubt be excellent students, if they were not already convinced of their own knowledge."

The lowly will inherit the land—heaven.

27 *"Blest are they who hunger and thirst for holiness / they shall have their fill."*
(Mt 5:6)

Holiness is achieved not by feverish activity, but by a humble submission to God's will.

We have an instinctive desire for goodness. As the hunger and thirst becomes stronger, it makes that desire for goodness sharper and more intense. It makes us more willing to put forth the effort and sacrifice that real goodness demands. We may never achieve the height of goodness to which we aspire, but our longing and desiring it with all our heart is acceptable to God.

28 *"Blest are they who show mercy; mercy shall be theirs."* (Mt 5:7)

Mercy and compassion are frequent themes in the gospel. Jesus reminds us that only if we forgive others will our heavenly Father forgive us (Mt 6:14). The reward of compassion is compassion, as James writes: "Merciless is the judgment on the man who has not shown mercy; but mercy triumphs over judgment" (Jas 2:13).

A French proverb says: "To know all is to forgive all." We need to know a person's mind and heart. Jesus had a contemplative insight into the dispositions of all who came to him.

29 *"Blest are the single-hearted for they shall see God."* (Mt 5:8)

This beatitude demands a most exacting examination. Jesus wants us to scrutinize our motives for what we do. It is difficult for us to have unmixed motives. Do we expect praise and thanks? Do we do all for the sake of Christ or for the sake of prestige? Do we relish acknowledgment or bask in the sunshine of self-approval? Even in prayer we may wish to be in the company of the Lord simply for his consolations or for the enjoyment of a pleasant feeling.

If our primary motive is to please God, then we are single-hearted.

30 *"Blest too are the peacemakers; they shall be called the sons of God."* (Mt 5:9)

A peacemaker is a person who tries to reconcile others who have become estranged from one another. Jesus set this forth clearly as our Christian duty (Mt 5:23-26). By peace we mean everything that makes for a person's highest good. A peacemaker tries to bridge gulfs, to heal breaches, to sweeten bitterness, to cement relationships.

Abraham Lincoln summed it up: "Die when I may, I would like it said of me, that I always pulled up a weed and planted a flower where I thought a flower would grow."

31 *"Blest are you when they insult you and persecute you and utter every kind of slander against you because of me. / Be glad and rejoice, for your reward is great in heaven."*

(Mt 5:11-12)

One of the outstanding qualities of Jesus was his absolute honesty. He never left people in any doubt as to what would happen to them if they chose to become one of his disciples. He never tried to trick anyone into following him. He said plainly: "They will harry you as they harried me" (Jn 15:20).

Jesus did not come to make life easy, but to make people great.

Fruits of the Spirit

J ESUS REDEEMED THE WHOLE human race by his passion, death, and resurrection. His redemption gained for us the capacity to receive his divine life. He himself told us of this fruit of his redeeming love: "I came / that they might have life / and have it to the full" (Jn 10:10).

However, the gifts of his redemption are not automatically applied to us. We must willingly accept and fulfill the conditions which Jesus laid down. Not everyone did so: "To his own he came, / yet his own did not accept him. / Any who did accept him / he empowered to become children of God" (Jn 1:11f).

We become the "children of God" in baptism when the Father adopts us as his daughters and sons and the Holy Spirit makes of us his temple. As the Sanctifier, the Holy Spirit dwells with us and within us. His presence is a dynamic, operative power purifying, energizing, and sanctifying us. He graciously bestows his gifts upon us. These gifts are far too many to enumerate. Paul speaks of some of these gifts of the Holy Spirit in 1 Cor 12:4ff; Eph 4:11ff; Rom 12:6ff. With our willing cooperation, these gifts will blossom forth into the fruit of the Spirit.

The scriptural quotations which follow for each day of the month should lead us into a deeper understanding of these fruit of the Spirit. These words of sacred scripture will give us some directives which will help us permit the fruit of the Spirit to come to full fruition in our lives.

"The fruit of the spirit is love, joy, peace, patient endurance, kindness, generosity, faith, mildness, and chastity" (Gal 5:22-23).

1 *The fruit of the spirit is love.* (Gal 5:22)

Love is listed as the first fruit of the Spirit. In fact, it embodies all the other fruit. The others are all component parts of love and spring from it in some way.

There are four different words used in Greek for our one word—love. *Eros* love has passion in it. *Philia* is the warm love we have for those nearest and dearest to us. *Storge* is the kind of affection parents and children have for one another. *Agape* is the highest form of love which exists between us and God.

Holy Spirit, fill us with your love and teach us how to love.

2 *The love of God has been poured out in our hearts through the Holy Spirit who has been given to us.* (Rom 5:5)

Agape is the Greek word we use to describe the special kind of love which the Holy Spirit pours into us. It is that kind of Christian love which transforms us to the extent that regardless of what another person may do to us we will never seek anything but that person's highest good.

It is a deliberate effort, which we cannot make without God's help, to seek nothing but the best, even for those who seek the worst for us. This is how Jesus loved.

3 *Out of love, place yourselves at one another's service.* (Gal 5:13)

Genuine love must give. Love impels us to seek good for others, to be vitally concerned about the welfare of our brothers and sisters in Christ, and to pursue a course which will be beneficial to them. Love urges us to give without counting the cost, to give without expecting a recompense or even an acknowledgment. Love discovers that there is more joy in giving than in receiving. That is love's reward.

4 *Over all these virtues put on love, which binds the rest together and makes them perfect.* (Col 3:14)

All virtues spring from love. They are all contained in the essence of love. Love must be the motivating force in all our good deeds; otherwise they would be empty and meaningless. It is not *what* we do, but *why* we do something that is all-important.

Our love for others will radiate and reflect the love of Jesus. Our love will find ways and means of encouraging, excusing, and empathizing with others. Be assured that same love will return to us.

5 *Your love must be sincere. Detest what is evil, cling to what is good. Love one another with the affection of brothers. Anticipate each other in showing respect.* (Rom 12:9-10)

Sincere love gives us insights beyond analysis. Love sees beyond externals. Love shows respect because it recognizes the image of God in another. Love makes us realize that we are all adopted daughters and sons of our common Father. This makes us true brothers and sisters to one another.

If human family ties are strong, how much stronger should be our spiritual bonds.

6 *"The fruit of the spirit is ... peace."* (Gal 5:22)

Peace is one of the special fruit of the Holy Spirit. By peace we do not mean merely freedom from fear, troubles, and disturbances. It is much more. It is rather a state of serenity of mind and heart. The Hebrew word *shalom* expresses it more adequately. In Hebrew it means that gift which brings a person the greatest possible good.

Peace is a tranquility of heart which is the fruit of an awareness that God loves us with an infinite love and that he cares for us at every moment of the day and night.

7 " 'Peace' is my farewell to you, / my peace is my
gift to you; / I do not give it to you as the world
gives peace." (Jn 14:27)

Jesus uses the word peace in all its
richness. He does not mean the popular
greeting or farewell. It is not the traditional
salutation—*shalom*. Peace is the gift of salvation. This is Jesus' solemn promise to us
the night before he died. From the moment
of his resurrection the Holy Spirit has been
shedding that peace upon us.

Thank you, Lord, for that peace which
the world cannot give.

8 "Peace be with you." (Jn 20:19, 21)

By his death and resurrection, Jesus won
that peace which only redemption can
bring. The awareness that we are forgiven
all of our sinfulness is the source of genuine
peace.

On the day of the resurrection, Jesus
twice greeted his apostles with "Peace be
with you." Through the power of the Holy
Spirit, we are filled with his peace. The
sacrament of penance is a channel in which
his peace is administered to us personally.

9 *"Better a dry crust with peace / than a house full of feasting with strife."* (Prv 17:1)

Peace is that gift of the Holy Spirit which we enjoy when we are satisfied with what we have and are. It makes no difference whether we are rich or poor, learned or unlettered, young or old.

When we are obsessed with a desire for something we do not have, or something we cannot do, we will not be at peace. On the other hand, when we rejoice with all the blessings and gifts God has so generously bestowed upon us, we will enjoy great peace.

May the peace of the Lord be with us always.

10 *The fruit of the spirit is . . . joy.* (Gal 5:22)

As a fruit of the Holy Spirit, joy is that interior delight which we experience from knowing that we are so loved by God that he has come to make his home in us through the power of the Holy Spirit.

His presence within us quells our restlessness. This quiet joy gladdens our hearts and makes us want to rejoice and praise God for all his goodness to us.

J stands for Jesus, O for nothing, and Y for you. If nothing stands between you and Jesus, you will have great joy.

11 *"All this I tell you / that my joy may be yours / and your joy may be complete."*
(Jn 15:11)

There is only one source of genuine joy—the good news that God loves us just as we are regardless of what we might have done. Jesus came into our world to prove in a concrete way that we are loved and lovable. He did so by revealing the gospel message to us. Can there be any greater cause for rejoicing?

12 *Rejoice instead, in the measure that you share Christ's sufferings. When his glory is revealed, you will rejoice exultantly.* (1 Pt 4:13)

Suffering is enveloped in mystery. It is sufficient to say that Jesus never asks us to suffer anything which he himself has not endured and thus sanctified. Our faith reminds us that there is purpose in suffering. Every pain, hardship, and misunderstanding helps us to mature spiritually. Even more, such suffering can serve as stepping stones into our union with the Lord.

13 *Rejoice in the Lord always! I say it again. Rejoice! Everyone should see how unselfish you are.* (Phil 4:4-5)

The Christian way of life must be joy-filled. Jesus set that criterion. Backslapping hilarity is not a manifestation of Christian joy. It may even be an escape. Christian joy is a deep, quiet peace which is reflected in our attitudes, appearance, and behavior.

We all know people whose very presence quietly, but deeply electrifies a whole group of people. We are likewise called to be examples of genuine Christian joy.

14 *The fruit of the spirit is . . . patient endurance.* (Gal 5:22)

John Chrysostom describes patient enurance as the quality of a person who could revenge himself and does not. A patient, enduring person is slow to anger and slow to speak. Jesus practiced patient endurance. When his enemies attacked him for his teaching, his healing, in fact for everything he did and said, he continued to reach out to them in love. His example is a compelling challenge for us.

15 *Realize that when your faith is tested this makes for endurance. Let endurance come to its perfection so that you may be fully mature and lacking in nothing.* (Jas 1:3-4)

In the process of maturing we may have to suffer some pain. Patient endurance is essential for our spiritual and emotional growth and development. The Holy Spirit endows us with the gifts of wisdom and understanding, enabling us to recognize the value of these trials and tribulations and to accept them with patient endurance.

16 *Be kind to one another, compassionate, and mutually forgiving, just as God has forgiven you in Christ.* (Eph 4:32)

In the New Testament, the expression "patient endurance" is frequently used to denote God's attitude toward us sinners. God's patience with us, in spite of our infidelities and lack of generous response to his love, is a proof of his mercy.

We are urged as followers of Jesus to strive for the same patient, enduring attitude.

17 *The fruit of the spirit. . . . is kindness.*
(Gal 5:22)

Kindness is an attribute of love and is also its motivating force. Kindness is recognizable as a fruit of the Holy Spirit by the radiant dispositions it engenders in a person. A kind person is a gentle, considerate, friendly person. A kind person has a forebearing nature and is interested in another's welfare.

Jesus was the kindest person who ever walked the face of the earth. As his followers, we must endeavor to walk in his footsteps.

18 *When he is dealing with the arrogant, he is stern, / but to the humble he shows kindness.* (Prv 3:34)

God wants to be a kind, gracious Father to us, but we must be disposed to receive his kindness. An arrogant person is often intoxicated with his own importance and self-worth, his own gifts and talents, so that he or she is not open and receptive to God's kindness.

When he told us of the Pharisee and the tax collector who went up to the temple to pray, Jesus capped it all with this caution: "For everyone who exalts himself shall be humbled while he who humbles himself shall be exalted" (Lk 18:14).

19 *Do you not know that God's kindness is an invitation to you to repent?* (Rom 2:4)

Jesus always radiated kindness. On one shameful occasion he displayed unusual kindness in dealing with his enemies. That occasion was during his trial before the Sanhedrin, Herod, and Pilate. Jesus remained silent, perhaps hoping that by his silence he would cause his judges to look within themselves to discover that they had no case against him and that they would accept his invitation to repent.

Our silence in similar circumstances would reflect this fruit of the Holy Spirit operative within us.

20 *The fruit of the spirit is . . . generosity.* (Gal 5:22)

There is a selfish streak in all of us. It is so easy to become concerned about self and forgetful of others. In order that we may become generous, we need the transforming power of the Holy Spirit. He can empower us to become magnanimous if we permit him. The Holy Spirit will endow us with a noble and forbearing spirit. We are called to become such a witness.

21 *It is in Christ and through his blood that we have been redeemed and our sins forgiven, so immeasurably generous is God's favor to us.* (Eph 1:7-8)

God has outdone himself in giving us Jesus as our Savior and Redeemer—so generous is his redeeming love. Generosity instills and inspires generosity. As we give ourselves ungrudgingly in loving service to family, friends, and neighbors, we are witnessing to the fruit of the Holy Spirit within us. Our generosity begets a generous spirit in others through which the Lord accomplishes his work on earth.

22 *If any of you is without wisdom, let him ask it from God who gives generously and ungrudgingly to all, and it will be given him.*
(Jas 1:5)

Wisdom guides and instructs us how to live as Jesus' disciples. We need the Holy Spirit's gift of wisdom to recognize and discern God's will concerning many occasions in our life. In his gracious generosity God will grant us the gift of wisdom if we sincerely seek it. Furthermore, his generosity will depend on how well we use the gifts which he gives us.

23 *The fruit of the spirit is . . . faith.* (Gal 5:22)

Faith, as a fruit of the Holy Spirit, makes us more dedicated and more trustworthy followers of the Lord. When we begin to realize how faithful God has been, is, and will continue to be, then we are inspired to be more faithful and generous in our response to his will and his love. Singing his praises will encourage greater fidelity to him.

Praise the Lord, all you nations;
    glorify him, all you peoples!
For steadfast is his kindness toward us
    and the fidelity of the Lord endures
    forever. (Ps 117)

24 *God is faithful, and it was he who called you to fellowship with his Son, Jesus Christ our Lord.* (1 Cor 1:9)

The Hebrews used the word *hesed* to describe the fidelity and trustworthiness of God. *Hesed* describes God better than any other word in our vocabulary.

In his faithfulness he called us to a unique and privileged relationship with him as our Father and into "fellowship with his Son." He adopted us as his daughters and his sons. He has surrounded us with his loving concern. Such fidelity elicits a greater trustworthiness from us, his children.

25 *For his trustworthiness and meekness /*
God selected him from all mankind.

(Sir 45:4)

We need models to challenge our way of life. The meekness and trustworthiness of Moses is a compelling example. We may not be asked to deliver a whole nation from slavery, but our mission is to encourage others to escape the slavery of sin and to return to the Lord, whose open arms on the cross offer mercy and forgiveness, pardon and peace.

James reminds us: "The person who brings a sinner back from his way will save his soul from death and cancel a multitude of sins" (Jas 5:20).

26 *The fruit of the spirit is ... mildness.*
(Gal 5:22-23)

Mildness is characteristic of a truly humble person. Such a person is always submissive to the will of God. A mild person is considerate and respectful of other people's needs and preferences. A mild person is a malleable person and not too proud to learn. Such a humble person can be taught and transformed by the Holy Spirit. A mild person is ever aware of Jesus' bidding: "Learn from me, for I am gentle and humble of heart" (Mt 11:29).

27 *Venerate the Lord, that is, Christ, in your hearts. Should anyone ask you the reason for this hope of yours, be ever ready to reply, but speak gently and respectfully.* (1 Pt 3:15-16)

The Holy Spirit can be compared to yeast. Yeast has power within itself, but it is not operative until it is placed into flour. There it works quietly. Likewise, the Holy Spirit has a divine power which is operative within us, working quietly and gently. In reaching out to others, we must also be gentle and respectful in proclaiming the good news more by living it rather than merely speaking about it.

28 *Your adornment is rather the hidden character of the heart, expressed in the unfading beauty of a calm and gentle disposition.* (1 Pt 3:4)

Although Peter was addressing himself to the early Christian women, his words apply to all of us. A good Christian must radiate the peace and joy of the Holy Spirit more by his or her attitudes and actions rather than simply by words.

We are the temples of the Holy Spirit. We must permit him to channel his love through us to others. "A calm and gentle disposition" is of paramount importance for this mission.

29 *The fruit of the spirit is . . . chastity.*
(Gal 5:22-23)

In our age, premarital sex, cohabitation, promiscuity, and adultery are not only being condoned, but even justified with reasons such as psychological need or self-fulfillment.

With the grace of the Holy Spirit we can better understand that chastity is not so much a denial of self-gratification as it is a positive way of giving ourselves to our loving Father. The Spirit shows us that every temptation is a golden opportunity to die to self and to give ourselves as a love-offering to the Lord. He shows us also the dignity of the sacredness of sex as coming from God's creative love.

30 *You shall not commit adultery. . . . You shall not covet your neighbor's wife.*
(Ex 20:14, 17)

These two commandments have come down through the ages unchanged and unaltered. The gospel reiterates and reinforces them because human nature does not change, nor does divine law.

Jesus went one step further: "What I say to you is: anyone who looks lustfully at a woman has already committed adultery with her in his thoughts" (Mt 5:28). Jesus was not speaking about passing thoughts: sin enters only when they are entertained.

31 *Make no mistake about it, no one makes a fool of God! A man will reap only what he sows. If he sows in the field of the flesh, he will reap a harvest of corruption; but if his seed-ground is the spirit, he will reap everlasting life.*
(Gal 6:7-8)

"As we sow, so shall we reap"—in his pastoral zeal Paul reminds us of this truth, with the encouragement to be open to the work of the Holy Spirit within. Quoting the Lord's message to him, he says: "My grace is enough for you, for in weakness power reaches perfection" (2 Cor 12:9).

Mary: An Example to Follow

IN PROPHECY AND PROMISE the Holy Spirit reveals the tender mercy and compassion of our loving Father for his sinful people. As the time was drawing near for the fulfillment of God's promises to send a Redeemer, the Holy Spirit presents Mary and her privileged role in salvation history. We begin our prayer this month with some reflections on the fulfillment of these prophecies, especially those concerned with the role of Mary, the mother of Jesus and our mother.

Next we turn to the gospel. In one brief, power-packed statement Jesus presents his mother to us: "There is your Mother" (Jn 19:27). Jesus gave us his mother as our model and exemplar. She is also our powerful intercessor in heaven. Surely, Mary has proved herself to be a loving, devoted, caring, concerned mother to all of us.

The next reflection centers on Mary's life of prayer. She was a person of profound prayer. Even the sparse mentions of her in scripture are sufficient to bring us into an appreciation of her prayerfulness. Her example impels us to realize the necessity of prayer in our own life. Mary's very lifestyle is truly a model and an ideal for our emulation.

Mary's prayer reached a height of ecstatic joy when her heart burst forth in her canticle of praise to the Father (Lk 1:46-55). In her Magnificat, Mary leads us into the first and foremost objective of prayer—praise, glory, and gratitude to God. During the final week of the month as we pray with her, may our hearts reverberate with that joy which only God can give.

1 *"I will put enmity between you and the woman, / and between your offspring and hers; / he will strike at your head, / while you strike at his heel."* (Gn 3:15)

After the fall of our first parents, God, in his infinite mercy and compassion, promised a Redeemer, a Savior, who would reconcile the human race with God again, who would mend and reestablish the fractured, fragmented relationship with our loving Father. Mary is the woman mentioned in this prophecy.

As Mary was chosen for this privileged role, we have been chosen by God for a very specific mission in life. Ask her to aid us in responding as graciously as she did.

2 *The Lord himself will give you this sign: the virgin shall be with child, and bear a son, and shall name him Immanuel.* (Is 7:14)

The sign which the Holy Spirit mentioned in this prophecy started a whole chain of the mighty and marvelous works of God. Through our Virgin Mother, Jesus brought life to our world. His suffering wrought our redemption; his resurrection brought new hope; his ascension a promise of heavenly glory.

Contemplating these mysteries, beginning with Mary's role, makes us want to sing the praise of God who worked these wonders because he loves us.

3 *Rejoice heartily, O daughter Zion, / shout for joy, O daughter Jerusalem! / See, your king shall come to you; a just savior is he.* (Zc 9:9)

During the long years of waiting for the coming of the promised Redeemer, the Holy Spirit reinforced the prophecies of a Savior who would bring peace and joy to an unredeemed people.

Reflecting on these events of salvation history should fill us with a greater spirit of gratitude for God's redemptive love being poured out upon us. As we hear these words in the liturgy of the word in the Mass honoring our Blessed Mother, we are reminded that we are a chosen people living in a privileged time. Let us "rejoice heartily and shout for joy."

4 *Who is this that comes forth like the dawn, / as beautiful as the moon, as resplendent as the sun?* (Sg 6:10)

The Song of Songs attempts to express the beauty of divine love. The liturgy of the church applies these words to our Blessed Mother. Mary is portrayed as the moon reflecting the light of the sun—her Son. This illustrates Mary's maternal care and concern for us, her children.

The moon dispels some of the darkness of night. By her example and lifestyle, by her powerful intercession, Mary helps to illumine our journey through life.

5 *When the designated time had come, God sent forth his Son born of a woman ... so that we might receive our status as adopted sons.*

(Gal 4:4-5)

Without mentioning Mary by name, Paul reminds us of God's fidelity to his promise of a Redeemer. Jesus coming through Mary made us the adopted daughters and sons of God. Mary, then, became our mother in a very special way. She is the mother of the body of Christ. She is the mother of the church. Thanks to Mary's fidelity, we can say: "Abba! Father!" because we have received "our status as adopted sons."

6 *Those he predestined he likewise called; those he called he also justified and those he justified, he in turn glorified.* (Rom 8:30)

In the liturgy the church applies these words to Mary. She was predestined, called, justified, and glorified. The fruits of the redemption were preapplied to her, keeping her a sinless habitation for the Son of God.

We, too, are called, justified as a result of Jesus' redemptive sacrifice. We will also be glorified. The Holy Spirit asks us to be cooperative so that we may receive the fullness of the fruits of the redemption.

7 *A great sign appeared in the sky, a woman clothed with the sun, with the moon under her feet, and on her head a crown of twelve stars.*
(Rv 12:1)

This vision of John symbolizes the transition from the Old to the New Testament. God's people of old gave birth to the Messiah, and the Israel of old became the new Israel, the church.

The church applies this scripture to Mary. Jesus is the sun, while Mary, reflecting his glory, is the moon. The twelve stars are the tribes of Israel, foreshadowing the apostles.

Rejoice in God's infinite goodness as the Holy Spirit reveals his plan for our salvation and reveals also Mary's role entitling her to be the mother of the church.

8 *"Why did you search for me? Did you not know I had to be in my Father's house?"*
(Lk 2:49)

Although the loss of Jesus in the Temple was of short duration, Mary experienced the pain of separation. She did not know whether she would see Jesus again.

This experience let her understand the emptiness and torment of a person who strays from Jesus because of sin. For this reason we pray: "Pray for us sinners now and at the hour of our death."

9 *He went down with them then, and came to Nazareth, and was obedient to them.*

(Lk 2:51)

Mary's presence in the home at Nazareth was of paramount importance. She was Jesus' first teacher. She was his prayer-companion as together they went to the synagogue to pray the prayers of their people. Together they pondered the great mysteries of God which were taking place in their lives.

Call upon Mary's powerful intercession to aid you as teacher, parent, or in any other walk of life to which you are called. Let her be your prayer-companion throughout life.

10 *During that time Jesus came from Nazareth in Galilee and was baptized in the Jordan by John.* (Mk 1:9)

When Jesus left home to begin his public ministry, Mary was not even mentioned. She knew that he would never again dwell in the hallowed peace and quiet of Nazareth. The pain of separation for Mary must have been acute.

Jesus gave us his mother that she might be our comfort and solace in the agonizing times of separation from a loved one.

11 *"Do whatever he tells you."* (Jn 2:5)

At the wedding feast at Cana, Jesus presented his mother in the role of a powerful intercessor. His hour had not yet come, yet he responded to his mother's wish.

For her part, Mary manifested her trust in Jesus. Without hesitation, she turned to the waiters with the instruction: "Do whatever he tells you." Her bidding to us is the same: "Do whatever God asks of you, and you will be blessed."

12 *"Rather, ... blest are they who hear the word of God and keep it."* (Lk 11:28)

Jesus explains that the true blessedness of his mother is not that she was chosen to be his mother, but rather that she heard the word of God, cherished it, prayed it, and lived it.

In God's sight our way of life is all-important. It is not what we seem to accomplish for him that pleases God, but rather how much we are concerned about living his word as Mary did. His word transforms our mind and heart so that we radiate the disposition and mentality of Jesus.

13 *Near the cross of Jesus there stood his mother.* (Jn 19:25)

Suffering is and always has been a mystery. A person in pain will often ask, why this suffering? Jesus not only gave us an example by accepting suffering himself, but he also gave us his mother as a perfect model. Mary *stood* near the cross. Her standing represented her total offering with that of her Son.

The gift of self in love is the source of joy in suffering.

14 *"Woman, there is your son. . . . There is your mother."* (Jn 19:26-27)

These words of Jesus manifest his loving concern for others even in the closing moments of his life on earth. In this brief statement he proclaimed his mother as the mother of the church and a special mother to us. When Jesus redeemed us, he incorporated us into his body. We form one body with him and Mary. Mary is the mother of the whole Christ, making her our mother, too.

May Mary help us to respond graciously and generously to the tremendous love of her Son for us.

15 *They took Jesus' body, and in accordance with the Jewish burial custom bound it up in wrappings of cloth with perfumed oils.*

(Jn 19:40)

The thirteenth station has been immortalized by Michelangelo's masterpiece the *Pieta.* How tenderly Mary must have accepted the lifeless body of Jesus into her arms. She must have touched every wound, every laceration as she tried to wipe away the dirt and spittle.

As the mother of the church, Mary takes into her arms all the wounded, suffering members of the body of Christ. Her maternal solicitude brings comfort, hope and encouragement to all who go to her.

16 *Together they devoted themselves to constant prayer. There were some women in their company, and Mary the mother of Jesus.*

(Acts 1:14)

Even though Jesus had already ascended into heaven, he wanted his mother to be known as the mother of the church. We find her with the infant church during that ten-day vigil of prayer, pleading for the outpouring of the Holy Spirit.

Today Mary prays with us and for us since we are members of the church. We belong especially to her.

17 *"How can this be since I do not know man?"* (Lk 1:34)

This question of Mary's does not reflect any hesitation on her part. Nor does it embody any fear, doubt, worry, or anxiety. It is really a prayer. Mary's chief concern was always to do the will of God perfectly in her life. By this question Mary was trying to ascertain just how she was to implement God's will in her life.

As soon as the angel explained, Mary's *fiat* followed immediately.

18 *"I am the servant of the Lord. Let it be done to me as you say."* (Lk 1:38)

Mary is our model and exemplar in many different areas of our spiritual life. She teaches us much about the proper dispositions for prayer. In prayer she had drawn very close to God; hence her acquiescence to God's will at the annunciation came readily and without reservation.

In prayer we keep our will in tune with God's will in which we find much peace.

19 *Mary treasured all these things and reflected on them in her heart.* (Lk 2:19)

Mary could not understand how the shepherds recognized her Son, nor how the angels came to announce his birth. God's ways in all of our lives are mysterious and awe-inspiring. Mary contemplated these events in her heart while she praised and thanked God for the miracle of his love. Our reflective prayer will lead us into the same prayer posture.

20 *His parents used to go every year to Jerusalem for the feast of the Passover, and when he was twelve they went up for the celebration as was their custom.* (Lk 2:41-42)

At first glance this passage may strike us as being purely historical. On second thought, Luke is really revealing Mary's fidelity to liturgical prayer. It was their custom to go annually to worship with their people. By her example, Mary leads us to appreciate our privilege of worshiping together as the people of God.

21 *His mother meanwhile kept all these things in memory.* (Lk 2:51)

When Mary and Joseph had lost Jesus for three days and then found him in the Temple, they did not understand Jesus' actions nor his words. But Mary recognized the mysterious ways of God and pondered them in her heart.

As we spend time in prayer, God's ways become clearer to us. We will discover great peace and joy in our acceptance of his ways.

22 *"Blest is the womb that bore you and the breasts that nursed you!"* (Lk 11:27)

Jesus must have been pleased with this compliment from the woman in the crowd. He responded by pointing to Mary's true blessedness in keeping the word of God. Augustine writes: "Indeed the blessed Mary certainly did the Father's will, and so it was for her a greater thing to have been Christ's disciple than to have been his Mother and she is more blessed in her discipleship than in her motherhood."

We can also be blessed as we respond with Mary's assistance to our call to discipleship.

23 *"Rather, blest are they who hear the word of God and keep it."* (Lk 11:28)

Obviously Jesus was pointing to the prayer of his mother as the ideal posture in listening to the word of the Lord. Mary was truly blest because she heard God's word and let it become the rule of her life. As we listen to God's word in quiet prayer and let it find a home in our heart, it will mold, shape, and transform us so that we, too, will be blest. His word is power-packed.

24 *She gave birth to a son—a boy destined to shepherd all the nations with an iron rod. Her child was caught up to God and to his throne.* (Rv 12:5)

This vision of John supports the role of Mary in the history of salvation. The role of Mary was already fulfilled at the time of John's writing; nevertheless it points to God's faithfulness in keeping his promises. It likewise reminds us of Mary's fidelity in responding to her special role in God's redemptive plan.

This consideration moves us into a spirit of gratitude and also serves to remind us that we must be willing to accept the gift of salvation by our generous cooperation.

The Magnificat

My being proclaims the greatness of the Lord,
my spirit finds joy in God my savior,
For he has looked upon his servant in her
lowliness;
all ages to come shall call me blessed.
God who is mighty has done great things for
me,
holy is his name;
His mercy is from age to age
on those who fear him.
He has shown might with his arm;
he has confused the proud in their inmost
thoughts.
He has deposed the mighty from their thrones
and raised the lowly to high places.
The hungry he has given every good thing,
while the rich he has sent empty away.
He has upheld Israel his servant,
ever mindful of his mercy;
Even as he promised our fathers,
promised Abraham and his descendants forever.

(Lk 1:46-55)

25 *"My being proclaims the greatness of the Lord." (Lk 1:46)*

Mary's whole being resonated with the overwhelming goodness of the Lord. Faithful to his repeated promises throughout the ages, God was about to send us the long-awaited Savior and Redeemer.

With her whole being Mary praised God, and her joy burst forth in this magnificent song, which we call her Magnificat. As we recall the greatness of the Lord in our life, our hearts, too, will sing his praises with joy.

26 *"My spirit finds joy in God my savior."* (Lk 1:47)

Genuine Christian joy is a fruit of the Holy Spirit. Since Mary was sinless, the Holy Spirit was dynamic and operative within her all her life. Her deep appreciation of God's redeeming love for sinful mankind was certainly a cause for joy.

Jesus reiterated the source of our joy when he told us that he was revealing the good news of our redemption so that our joy might be complete (Jn 15:11).

With Mary let us rejoice in God our Savior.

27 *"For he has looked upon his servant in her lowliness; / all ages to come shall call me blessed."* (Lk 1:48)

Mary was truly blessed because of her unquestioning obedience to God's will and her total trust in his power to accomplish in her whatever he willed. This is an ideal prayer posture, realizing as Jesus said that without him we can do nothing, but with him we can do all things.

This is the path Mary points out to us.

28 *"God who is mighty has done great things for me, / holy is his name."* (Lk 1:49)

Genuine humility is based on truth—the truth about ourselves and the truth about God. Mary attributed all that was happening to her to the mighty power of God. She accepted no accolades nor claimed any credit for herself.

As the Lord wrought his power through Mary because of her receptivity, so he will accomplish great things in us and through us to others. Genuine humility is the key which unlocks the fountain of God's blessings for us.

29 *"His mercy is from age to age / on those who fear him."* (Lk 1:50)

Sin is a refusal to love. Throughout history the human race consistently turned away from God and rejected his love, yet his merciful love was always extended to anyone who turned to him. God's merciful compassion reached its zenith when he sent his Son, Jesus, into our sinful world as its Redeemer. In doing so he kept his promise: "My love shall never leave you" (Is 54:10).

30 *"He has shown might with his arm; / he has confused the proud in their inmost thoughts. / He has deposed the mighty from their thrones / and raised the lowly to high places."*
(Lk 1:51-52)

The proud are intoxicated with their own self-sufficiency. They use their God-given gifts as though they were personally responsible for them. Their humanistic ideals have become their neon, plastic god. Like the Pharisee in the Temple (Lk 18:9), they are not open to the working of God's power in them.

In contrast, God's divine power worked marvels and wonders in Mary because of her lowliness and humility.

31 *"The hungry he has given every good thing, / while the rich he has sent empty away."*
(Lk 1:53)

There is within each one of us a longing, a hunger, a restlessness, which can be satisfied only when we have the reassurance that we are loved and accepted by God. Only God can and does satisfy this hunger.

However, one all-important condition is necessary. We must be open and receptive to the Lord by humbly and trustingly presenting ourselves to him so that his will may be accomplished in us.

Once again, Mary shows us the way. "To Jesus through Mary."

Living with Our Eucharistic Lord

ONE OF THE MOST COMFORTING and consoling truths for us in this land of exile is the reassurance that Jesus gave us when he promised to remain with us always. He made that solemn promise to us, and he is forever faithful to his word. We are living with the risen Jesus. We need to remind ourselves constantly of his abiding presence.

This is the theme suggested for this month's prayer. For the first part of the month, the scriptures recall Jesus' promise and the fulfillment of that promise down through the ages. "Jesus Christ is the same yesterday, today, and forever" (Heb 13:8).

Jesus gave us concrete and positive proof of his abiding presence when he instituted the Holy Eucharist. In the Eucharist Jesus adapted himself to our human limitations, using signs and symbols of his presence— bread and wine. In the eucharistic celebration we are reminded of the forgiving, healing love of the Lord. We have the occasion to thank and praise him before he gives us the sustaining, nourishing gift of himself in Holy Communion. In conclusion he asks us to become Eucharist to others.

During the last week of the month, we will contemplate an episode from the gospel which depicts his abiding presence— the encounter of Jesus with the two disciples on the road to Emmaus. Like the disciples, we make our daily trek to Emmaus, be it at home, at work, on a shopping tour, or visiting family or friends. Jesus is accompanying us all day long.

In the Emmaus account we also find some parallels with the Mass. In our prayer time we will discover even more.

1 *"I will not leave you orphaned; / I will come back to you."* (Jn 14:18)

The most powerful antidote for loneliness is to know that Jesus loves us so much that he never leaves us but remains with us always. This is the solemn promise he made to us in the upper room the night before he died. He is abiding with us and within us. As we respond to his love, we form a deep personal union with him. There is no better cure!

2 *"Know that I am with you always, until the end of the world."* (Mt 28:20)

Jesus is our constant companion, living with us in his resurrected life as we proceed down life's highway. He lightens our burden when it seems too heavy for us. He fills us with the peace and joy which only he can give. As Christians our privilege is unique and tremendous. Spending some time each day with the Lord will increase our own love and gratitude to God.

3 *"Anyone who loves me, / will be true to my word, / and my Father will love him; / and we will come to him / and make our dwelling place with him."* (Jn 14:23)

Human love seeks a deep, personal bond of unity with the beloved so that eventually two hearts will beat in unison.

Divine love, already in this world, forms an even greater bond of unity to be augmented and fulfilled in heaven where we will share in the divine life of the Holy Trinity. The fact that God makes his dwelling place with us in this life is already a foretaste of the community of perfect love which God has for us in heaven.

4 *You must know that your body is a temple of the Holy Spirit, who is within—the Spirit you have received from God.* (1 Cor 6:19)

Our baptism is one of the most important occasions in our lives. At that precise moment the Holy Spirit comes to dwell with us, making us his special temple. He remains with us all the days of our life. At that moment, too, the Father adopts us as his sons and daughters. In a very real sense, we become brothers and sisters to one another. We are already entering into the vestibule of heaven where we will be more intimately united in the perfect love of the Holy Trinity.

5 *You are the temple of the living God. . . . "I will dwell with them and walk among them. / I will be their God / and they shall be my people."*
(2 Cor 6:16)

These words are spoken by the transcendent God of heaven and earth, the Creator and Sustainer of the entire universe. His love for us is so infinite that he wants to dwell with us and walk with us down life's pathway. Our dignity is sublime. Our mission is to permit him to radiate his goodness through us as we journey up and down the hills and valleys of daily living.

6 *The life I live now is not my own; Christ is living in me.* (Gal 2:20)

Jesus rose from the dead that he might share his divine, risen life with us. His unique presence is indeed a wondrous mystery. By his divine presence, Jesus energizes and stimulates us to reach out in greater loving concern for others. We discover that we are capable of doing certain things which we never thought were possible. His divine life transforms and sustains us, thus enabling him to touch others through us.

Lord, keep me aware of your life in me!

7 *This is God's dwelling among men. He shall dwell with them and they shall be his people and he shall be their God who is always with them.* (Rv 21:3)

Basking in the presence of the Lord and enjoying the touch of his love as it nourishes, warms, and fills us is only a feeble attempt to visualize the joy and happiness that awaits us in heaven. How well the inspired word of God says: "Eye has not seen, ear has not heard, / nor has it so much as dawned on man / what God has prepared for those who love him" (1 Cor 2:9).

All the other joys will be God's eternal surprise.

8 *"I will be his God and he shall be my son."* (Rv 21:7)

In describing the new Jerusalem, heaven, the Father reveals a Father-child relationship. He will be our Father, and we are his sons and daughters. A family relationship is only a poor image of what God has in store for us. God could tell us no more because our finite minds could not comprehend it, nor can words explain the bliss that awaits us.

9 *The doors of heaven he opened; / He rained manna upon them for food / and gave them heavenly bread.* (Ps 78:23-24)

The Israelites were desperate for food in the desert. Their very survival depended upon it. Poetically and prophetically the psalmist relates the miracle of God's love—bread from heaven.

We, too, are on our journey toward heaven—our promised land. Our plight is equally urgent. We need sustenance to ensure the completion of our journey. Jesus fulfilled this prophecy with the gift of himself in the Eucharist. Again "the doors of heaven" are opened to rain down, not manna, but the Lord himself.

10 *"I myself am the bread of life. / No one who comes to me shall ever be hungry, / no one who believes in me shall ever thirst."* (Jn 6:35)

Using the title, "bread of life," Jesus is telling us that in the Eucharist he can be the total fulfillment of life. He selected bread and wine as the signs and symbols of his abiding presence with us. He lives with us and within us to care for our every need. He summarizes all our needs under the caption of food and drink. Then he assures us that if we come to him, we shall never be hungry, and if we really believe in him, we shall never be thirsty.

11 *"He who feeds on my flesh / and drinks my blood / has eternal life / and I will raise him up on the last day."* (Jn 6:54)

When Jesus rose from the dead, he enjoyed a risen, exalted, glorified life. It is this life he shares with us at baptism when we become the temples of the Holy Spirit. He implements that life within us each time we receive him in the Eucharist. The Eucharist is the pledge of that fullness of life which will be ours in eternity. Jesus makes this generous promise when he says: "I will raise him up on the last day."

12 *"I have greatly desired to eat this Passover with you before I suffer."* (Lk 22:15)

Jesus reveals the longing of his heart to make the gift of himself to us in the Eucharist. He did so at the Last Supper and continues to do so each time we offer the Eucharist with him. As we approach the altar, we can hear the same words: "I have greatly desired to celebrate this Mass with you and to offer your gifts along with the gift of myself to the Father."

We are a privileged people!

13 *"This is my body to be given for you. Do this as a remembrance of me."* (Lk 22:19)

Jesus invites us, not merely to offer the Eucharist, but to bring to the Eucharist what he brought—the gift of his whole life.

Our gift, represented by the bread and wine, is perfected by Jesus, our eternal High Priest, and presented to the Father in our name. There is no more perfect way of adoring, praising, thanking, and petitioning our Father than through and with Jesus at Mass. That is why Jesus is so anxious to have us do what he did.

14 *"This is my body to be given for you. . . . This cup is the new covenant in my blood, which will be shed for you."* (Lk 22:19-20)

With these few earthshaking words Jesus gave us the gift of himself as Redeemer and Savior. In this eucharistic gift he embodied the whole mystery of redemption and salvation. This mystery began to unfold with the manna in the desert. His victory on the cross brought it to fulfillment. This is incorporated and re-presented in every Mass.

> How shall I make a return to the Lord
>   for all the good he has done for me?
> The cup of salvation I will take up,
>   and I will call upon the name of the
>   Lord. (Ps 116:12-13)

15 *The grace of the Lord Jesus Christ, and the love of God, and the fellowship of the Holy Spirit be with you all!* (2 Cor 13:13)

This prayerful greeting at the beginning of Mass is used many times by Paul in his Letters. It is easy to understand its popularity. It is all-inclusive. We address ourselves to the Holy Trinity, begging the Lord Jesus for his grace and gifts, reminding ourselves of the infinite, paternal love of the Father, and likewise recalling the abiding, dynamic presence of the Holy Spirit within us. It is an ideal prayer with which to begin the eucharistic celebration.

16 *"Father, I have sinned against God and against you; I no longer deserve to be called your son."* (Lk 15:18)

Many of us, recognizing our own waywardness, can identify with the prodigal son. If our spirit of humble repentance is as sincere as his, the Father receives us with arms outstretched.

As we enter into the penitential rite, this should be the disposition of our hearts. As we approach the presence of the Lord in the Eucharist, we can see our own faults and failures in a clearer light.

Lord, have mercy.

17 *"O God, be merciful to me, a sinner."*
(Lk 18:13)

This humble contrite prayer of the tax collector in the Temple set the tone and disposition which should be ours as we begin the Mass.

Jesus' comment is also meant for us: "Believe me, this man went home from the Temple justified but the other did not" (Lk 18:14).

We too can go home from Mass justified if our heart is the same as the tax collector.

18 *"Glory to God in high heaven, / peace on earth to those on whom his favor rests."*
(Lk 2:14)

In the eucharistic celebration at times, we join in the refrain of the angels in the shepherds' field praising God. Praise is the highest form of vocal prayer. We owe God our praise, honor, and glory. As we praise the Lord, our souls are filled with joy and jubilation. At the Eucharist we praise God especially for his Son Jesus as Savior, Redeemer, High Priest.

19 *"I do believe! Help my lack of trust!"* (Mk 9:24)

With these same sentiments we make our own profession of faith at liturgies on Sundays and solemnities. Our profession of faith is not merely giving intellectual assent to a carefully compiled set of doctrines. It is also expressing our fervent desire to want to live them. How pleased our Father must be when we pray: "I do believe! Help me to live accordingly."

20 *"Holy, holy, holy is the Lord of hosts! ... All the earth is filled with his glory."* (Is 6:3)

"Blessed is he who comes in the name of the Lord! / Hosanna in the highest!" (Mt 21:9)

At the conclusion of the Preface of the Mass, we are invited to unite our voices with the choirs of angels to praise and magnify our God of power and might. We recognize how inadequate our own praise is, but we appreciate the joy of belonging to the body of Christ, especially the celestial choir in praising God. What joy should fill our hearts as we are privileged to unite our praise and thanksgiving with the whole church and thus reach the throne of God.

21 *"In him we live and move and have our being."* (Acts 17:28)

Jesus reminds us also that without him we can do nothing, which is just another way of saying that with him we can do all things.

In the Mass we recognize our own inadequacy and we praise God through our eucharistic Lord. This doxology concludes the Eucharistic Prayer before we begin the Communion Rite. Let our hearts rejoice as we sing: "Through him, with him, in him, in the unity of the Holy Spirit, all glory and honor is yours, almighty Father, forever and ever."

22 *"Look! There is the Lamb of God / who takes away the sin of the world."* (Jn 1:29)

Unblemished lambs were the victims offered in the sacrifices in the Temple. These lambs were selected from the flocks around Bethlehem, which is noteworthy since Jesus, the Lamb of God, was born there. These sacrifices were symbolic of the true sacrifice of the Lamb of God. Like the gentle Lamb, Jesus laid down his life for us. Before approaching him in Holy Communion we pray: "Lamb of God, you take away the sins of the world, have mercy on us."

23 *"Sir, do not trouble yourself, for I am not worthy to have you enter my house."*

(Lk 7:6)

The centurion showed great respect for Jesus. Even though he was a proud Roman officer, he did not consider himself worthy to receive Jesus as a guest into his home. The church has immortalized the words of this humble centurion as we pray with the same sentiments before Holy Communion. Lord, we are not worthy that you should come to us, but, like the centurion, we need you and expect great things from you.

24 *Is not the bread we break a sharing in the body of Christ? Because the loaf of bread is one, we, many though we are, are one body, for we all partake of one loaf.* (1 Cor 10:16-17)

The Eucharist is the sacrament of unity. Since we share his divine life, we are members of his body. We are the people of God. We are in reality sisters and brothers to each other. Jesus' coming to each one of us gives us even more solidarity. The matrix which binds us together is love. Jesus fills us with his love, thus uniting us to himself and enabling us to share his love with others.

May we be identified as were the early Christians: "See how they love one another."

The Road to Emmaus

Before entering into prayer for the next few days, it would be very profitable to read Luke's account of the two disciples on the road to Emmaus (Lk 24:13-35).

Two of them that same day were making their way to a village named Emmaus seven miles distant from Jerusalem, discussing as they went all that had happened. In the course of their lively exchange, Jesus approached and began to walk along with them. However, they were restrained from recognizing him. He said to them, "What are you discussing as you go your way?" They halted, in distress, and one of them, Cleopas by name, asked him, "Are you the only resident of Jerusalem who does not know the things that went on there these past few days?" He said to them, "What things?" They said: "All those that had to do with Jesus of Nazareth, a prophet powerful in word and deed in the eyes of God and all the people; how our chief priests and leaders delivered him up to be condemned to death, and crucified him. We were hoping that he was the one who would set Israel free. Besides all this, today, the third day since these things happened, some women of our group have just brought us some astonishing news. They were at the tomb before dawn and failed to find his body, but returned with the tale that they had seen a vision of angels who declared he was alive. Some of our number went to the tomb and found it to be just as the women said, but him they did not see."

Then he said to them, "What little sense you have! How slow you are to believe all that the prophets have announced! Did not the Messiah have to undergo all this so as to enter into his glory?" Beginning, then, with Moses and all the prophets, he interpreted for them every passage of Scripture which referred to him. By now they were near the village to which they were going, and he acted as if he were going farther. But they pressed him: "Stay with us. It is nearly evening— the day is practically over." So he went in to stay with them.

When he had seated himself with them to eat, he took bread, pronounced the blessing, then broke the bread and began to distribute it to them. With that their eyes were opened and they recognized him; whereupon he vanished from their sight. They said to one another, "Were not our hearts burning inside us as he talked to us on the road and explained the Scriptures to us?" They got up immediately and returned to Jerusalem, where they found the Eleven and the rest of the company assembled. They were greeted with, "The Lord has been raised! It is true! He has appeared to Simon." Then they recounted what had happened on the road and how they had come to know him in the breaking of bread.

25 *Jesus approached and began to walk with them. However, they were restrained from recognizing him.* (Lk 24:15-16)

Each day we make our own journey to Emmaus. We may be going to our place of work or business; it may be right in our own home, or wherever the Lord may lead us. Jesus is always with us and within us, even though we may not be consciously aware of his abiding presence. He remains with us to encourage and inspire, to console and comfort, to strengthen and enlighten us throughout the course of the day.

Let us rejoice that we are never alone.

26 *"What little faith you have! How slow you are to believe all that the prophets have announced!"* (Lk 24:25)

We are aware of Jesus' presence especially at Mass. There are some parallels between the Mass and the happenings on the road to Emmaus. Like the disciples, we may permit the events of the day to dishearten or disappoint us. We easily forget that whatever takes place in our lives somehow fits into God's plan for us.

We can bring these shortcomings to Jesus in the penitential rite of Mass. There we hear Jesus say to us: "What little faith you have! But I forgive you anyway."

27 *Beginning, then, with Moses and all the prophets, he interpreted for them every passage of Scripture which referred to him.*

(Lk 24:27)

As Jesus explained the scriptures to the disciples, so he does at the liturgy of the word at Mass. As we listen to his word, he will instruct and guide us. He will show us how to live his way of life in the happenings of every day. His word has the power to mold and transform our minds and hearts. From his word we derive a peace and joy which this world cannot give. Furthermore, he is present in his word.

28 *"Stay with us. It is nearly evening—the day is practically over." So he went in to stay with them.* (Lk 24:29)

Jesus is always a gentleman. He respects our free will. He never forces himself upon us. He has given us a free will to want him, to long for him, to desire him. He waited until the disciples invited him before he went in to stay with them. Likewise, he waits for our invitation. We can invite him to pray with us, to guide our deliberations at a meeting, to be present at our family gatherings, to assist us in difficulties. Be assured he is waiting for our invitation.

29 *He took bread, pronounced the blessing, then broke the bread and began to distribute it to them. With that their eyes were opened and they recognized him.* (Lk 24:30-31)

The Eucharist is a great mystery. Only divine love could have devised such a celestial gift. Truly he is Emmanuel: God-with-us. However, his presence is a hidden presence. The disciples were restrained from recognizing him. We likewise, can behold him only with eyes of faith. When Jesus asked the apostles if they could accept this mystery, Peter answered for all of us: "Lord, to whom shall we go? You have the words of eternal life" (Jn 6:68).

30 *"Were not our hearts burning inside us as he talked to us on the road and explained the Scriptures to us?"* (Lk 24:32)

Jesus is present in his word. It is not a static presence, but a dynamic, operative presence. His word energizes us and keeps our hearts burning within us, making us eager to know him better and to bring others to this same knowledge. His word fills us with peace and joy. In fact, Jesus told us that he revealed his word to us so that his joy may be ours and our joy may be complete. He asks only for a listening heart.

31 *They got up immediately and returned to Jerusalem . . . . They recounted what had happened on the road and how they had come to know him in the breaking of the bread.*

(Lk 24:33-35)

The disciples were so thrilled at seeing Jesus alive that they rushed all the way back to Jerusalem to share the good news with their community. This, too, has a parallel in every Mass.

At the end of Mass we are commissioned to "Go in peace to love and serve the Lord." Jesus has come as Eucharist to us, and now we are sent out to bring the fruits of that Eucharist to others.

From Life to Life

WE ARE ON OUR JOURNEY to the promised land. At times traveling may be difficult, even dangerous. It is tiresome to say the least. Jesus has clearly mapped out the way for us. Caution signs point out the likely pitfalls. The divine promise of eternal life empowers us to pursue our journey upward and onward.

We are never traveling alone. Jesus is our constant companion. Just as he accompanied the two disciples on the road to Emmaus, so he promised to be with us until the end of time.

In the following pages he speaks words of encouragement and reassurance, of hope and promise. Listen to his message for each day. Make it the watchword and theme for your reflection throughout the day. It will make your climb more gradual and gentle. His presence in his word will make the valleys seem less deep and the hills a bit lower. Above all, being overshadowed with the sunshine of love will make our journeying joyous and pleasant.

1 *Athirst is my soul for God, the living God. /*
When shall I go and behold the face of God?
(Ps 42:3)

At times life may seem rather empty and meaningless. We may become so frustrated and discouraged that we hover on the brink of giving up hope. The Lord may permit these feelings to help us keep our focus on him. There is a restlessness and a longing within us that only he can satisfy. It may be some time before we "behold the face of God," but with his grace we can see his will and his presence in all the happenings of life.

2 *You have preserved my life / from the pit of*
destruction, / when you cast behind your back
/ all my sins. (Is 38:17)

The Father's merciful, compassionate, forgiving love was proclaimed by the prophets down through the centuries. Jesus came as a concrete expression of a forgiving, healing, redeeming love that leads to salvation. Jesus assures us that he not only casts our sins behind his back, but that he has forgiven and forgotten all about them.

3 *The Lord is our savior; / we shall sing to stringed instruments / In the house of the Lord / all the days of our life.* (Is 38:20)

The angel of God brought "tidings of great joy to be shared by the whole people" when he announced: "This day in David's city a savior has been born to you" (Lk 2:10-11). The consciousness and the constant awareness that we are a redeemed and saved people will make us a happy and joyful people. God's will can best be accomplished in us if our hearts are filled with joy. Let our hearts, therefore, sing "all the days of our life."

4 *"Come. You have my Father's blessing! Inherit the kingdom prepared for you from the creation of the world."* (Mt 25:34)

Jesus' invitation to the blessed came as a joyful surprise. To their way of thinking they did not do anything extraordinary. Jesus reminded them that they had fulfilled the great commandment of love by acts such as feeding the hungry. We are called to reach out in loving service to others with the assurance that Jesus accepts our ministrations as done personally to him.

5 *"Out of my sight, you condemned, into that everlasting fire prepared for the devil and his angels!"* (Mt 25:41)

The words of Jesus seem harsh and the condemnation "of those on his left" severe until we recall that they refused to fulfill the two greatest commandments—love of God and love of neighbor. Their guilt must have arisen, not from a simple omission, but from self-centered malice and an on-going attitude of self-centeredness.

Our love for others will deliver us from condemnation and assure us of an inheritance in the kingdom.

6 *Yes, God so loved the world / that he gave his only Son, / that whoever believes in him may not die / but may have eternal life.* (Jn 3:16)

In this brief statement John is relating the greatest love story in human history. Sin estranged man from God. The chasm between God and our sinful human nature could not be spanned. Our sinful human nature did not have the capacity nor the potential to receive divine life. Human nature needed redemption.

God responded to our need by giving us his Son, Jesus, as our Savior and Redeemer. Even though we cannot comprehend such love with our human limitations, our acceptance in faith will bring us the fruits of his redeeming love—eternal life.

7 *The Father loves the Son / and has given everything over to him. / Whoever believes in the Son / has life eternal.* (Jn 3:35-36)

In these words Jesus was revealing his own divinity by asserting his oneness with the Father and the Holy Spirit. If we accept Jesus and his way of life, we are also accepting the whole Godhead. This faith, lived out in our daily life, is a sure path to eternal life.

I want to believe, Lord. Remove all my doubts which plague me from time to time.

8 *"I solemnly assure you, / the man who hears my word / and has faith in him who sent me / possesses eternal life. / He does not come under condemnation, / but has passed from death to life."* (Jn 5:24)

When we listen to the word of Jesus, what do we hear? Jesus reveals the truth that the Father loves us with an infinite love—a creating, caring, forgiving, enduring love. When we permit his word to find a home in our hearts, and when we have enough faith to take his word at face value, we do possess eternal life, and we will pass from death to life.

9 *"All that the Father gives me shall come to me; / no one who comes will I ever reject."* (Jn 6:37)

We may become unduly concerned and worried that our faults and failings, our self-centeredness and sinfulness may have erected an impenetrable barrier to our friendship and union with the Lord. In his dealing with the criminal on the cross, Jesus made it perfectly clear that he looks only at our heart and our disposition, not at our past record. Listen again as Jesus says: "No one who comes will I ever reject."

10 *"Indeed, this is the will of my Father, / that everyone who looks upon the Son / and believes in him / shall have eternal life. / Him I will raise up on the last day."* (Jn 6:40)

When Jesus uses the words "looks upon the Son," he does not mean a casual glance or just a momentary observing of him. No, he is speaking about gazing upon the Lord to observe him, to study him, to contemplate him.

Paul tells us that as we gaze upon the Lord's glory, we ourselves are being transformed (2 Cor 3:18). We become what we contemplate. As we contemplate Jesus, we become like him. As we become like him, we will have eternal life and he will raise us up on the last day.

11 *"I came / that they might have life / and have it to the full."* (Jn 10:10)

In order to give us the fullness of life, Jesus assumed our human nature and redeemed it, giving us the capacity to receive his divine life. During our earthly sojourn we receive his divine life in a limited way. When we pass through the doorway of death, we shall receive his divine life and love in all its fullness.

Jesus, we are glad you came.

12 *"My sheep hear my voice. / I know them, / and they follow me. / I give them eternal life, / and they shall never perish."* (Jn 10:27-28)

If a sheep is docile and follows the shepherd, he will be well fed and protected. He will have a good life. No danger will threaten him. If we recognize and listen to the voice of our Shepherd and follow his way of life, we will have not only a good life here, but life eternal. As the Good Shepherd, Jesus leads us. He walks with us. He never asks us to walk alone. With him at our side we shall never perish.

13 *"I am the resurrection and the life: / whoever believes in me, / though he should die, will come to life; / and whoever is alive and believes in me / will never die."* (Jn 11:25-26)

No promise can bring greater peace and joy into our lives than the divine promise of Jesus that, if we believe, we will live with him forever. Our resurrection is possible because of his resurrection. He rose from the dead because he loves us. Furthermore, our life with him will be a union of perfect love. Such loving reassurance makes us a happy people radiating the love, peace, and joy of the Lord along the pathway of life.

14 *Eternal life is this; / to know you, the only true God, / and him whom you have sent, Jesus Christ.* (Jn 17:3)

We can love a person intimately only when we know that person intimately. Only when we come to know God as our loving Father and Jesus as our caring, concerned Savior can our love grow and mature. Also, when we truly love a person, we will want to do all in our power to please our loved one. Such a love for God translated into action ensures us eternal life.

15 *Despite the increase of sin, grace has far surpassed it, so that, as sin reigned through death, grace may reign by way of justice leading to eternal life, through Jesus Christ our Lord.* (Rom 5:20-21)

When we look at the world around us, we are dismayed and disheartened at the depravity and the lack of moral standards. Nothing seems sacred. Surely we have lost our sense of sin. Despite this avalanche of evil and sin, God's patient mercy and compassion, his grace and goodness, rise far above the toll of evil. Such overwhelming kindness influences us to walk more deeply in his ways.

16 *If we have been united with him through likeness to his death, so shall we be through a like resurrection.* (Rom 6:5)

Love is a mystery. We cannot define it. We cannot understand it on this side of heaven, yet we enjoy loving and being loved with all the blessings it brings us. Jesus loves us so much that he united our unredeemed human nature with his, took it down into death with himself and redeemed it along with his own rising from the dead. His love has made us citizens of heaven. His love awaits our response.

17 *The wages of sin is death, but the gift of God is eternal life in Christ our Lord.*
(Rom 6:23)

Sin is a refusal to love God enough to do what he asks of us. It is also a refusal to accept God's love. When we willfully turn away from God, there is only one alternative: "the wages of sin is death." Despite our sinfulness, God continues his gifts of pardon, peace, joy, and happiness in this life and eternal bliss in the world to come.

18 *Now that you are freed from sin and have become slaves of God, your benefit is sanctification as you tend toward eternal life.*
(Rom 6:22)

Freedom from sin makes us the dwelling of the Holy Trinity. We "become slaves of God." Just as a slave belongs exclusively to his master, we, too, belong exclusively to God. In former times masters loved their servants (Lk 7). In turn, the slave loved his master and tried to do everything to please him. Our goal is the same. What can we do today as an expression of our love for our Master?

19 *Just as in Adam all die, so in Christ all will come to life again.* (1 Cor 15:22)

Before Adam's sin our eternal union with God would have been as natural as meeting a loved one. Sin brought disruption and death. Jesus conquered death and made death the transition from a temporal life replete with pain and sorrow into a life of eternal peace and happiness. Little wonder in the Easter Vigil the church sings, "O happy fault, O necessary sin of Adam, which gained for us so great a Redeemer."

20 *"Death is swallowed up in victory. O death, where is your victory? O death, where is your sting?"* (1 Cor 15:54-55)

Death is not so much the tearing asunder of our soul from our body as it is a freeing of our spirit to receive the divine life in all its fullness. There is no victory for death since it is the gateway projecting us into eternal glory. Jesus has also taken the sting out of death by his remaining with us through it all. Jesus' promise to stay with us always has also removed the loneliness we dread in death.

21 *The present burden of our trial is light enough, and earns for us an eternal weight of glory beyond all comparison.* (2 Cor 4:17)

With pastoral solicitude, Paul reminds us that the trials and tribulations, the hardships and sufferings of this life are a means of conditioning us by keeping our vision fixed on the heavenly glory to come. The weight of "the present burden" will be diminished in proportion to the love which motivates us. Furthermore, each trial can be a love-offering made to God whose response is "glory beyond all comparison."

22 *It is owing to his favor that salvation is yours through faith. This is not your doing, it is God's gift; neither is it a reward for anything you have accomplished, so let no one pride himself on it.* (Eph 2:8-9)

How much and how many of us are still obsessed with the idea that we must merit, earn, and deserve our heavenly reward? We regard God as the divine bookkeeper instead of a gracious Father. But salvation is God's gift to us. We must willingly, humbly, and gratefully accept his gift and cooperate with it by permitting his divine life to be operative within us.

A grateful person is solicitous about using a gift well.

23 *He will give a new form to this lowly body of ours and remake it according to the pattern of his glorified body, by his power to subject everything to himself.* (Phil 3:21)

After his resurrection, Jesus appeared in his glorified body. It was a mysterious existence. "Despite the locked doors, Jesus came and stood before them" (Jn 20:26).

After death we shall possess the same glorified, exalted life. Our curiosity longs to penetrate the mysterious existence awaiting us in the next world. Then we hear Jesus say, "I am the resurrection and the life.... Do you believe this?" (Jn 11:25-26).

24 *He [Jesus] has robbed death of its power and has brought life and immortality into clear light through the gospel.* (2 Tm 1:10)

The gospel message rejoices with the astounding news of Jesus' conquest of sin and death. As gold nuggets interspersed in the gospel, Jesus tells us something of the "why" of this overwhelming love:

I came / that they might have life / and have it to the full. (Jn 10:10)

There is no greater love that this: / to lay down one's life for one's friends.

(Jn 15:13)

Lord, keep me aware of your love.

25 *He himself made us a promise / and the promise is no less than this: / eternal life.*
(1 Jn 2:25)

Jesus is always faithful to his promises. He promised us eternal life. This is pure gift. We cannot earn it. We do not deserve it. Why, then, would Jesus make such an extravagant promise to us? There is one reason only: He loves us and wants us to be with him.

Listen to Jesus' fervent prayer: "Father, / all those you gave me / I would have in my company / where I am, / to see this glory of mine" (Jn 17:24).

26 *God gave us eternal life, / and this life is in his Son. / Whoever possesses the Son / possesses life.* (1 Jn 5:11-12)

At different times and in various ways, Jesus told us that he would remain with us and within us. We are his dwelling place. He empowers us "to become the children of God." When we welcome him by living our life in conformity with his way of life, then we are putting on the new man who is Jesus, and we also have the mind of Christ in us.

Possessing eternal life already in this world means we are living in the vestibule of heaven.

27 *Persevere in God's love, and welcome the mercy of our Lord Jesus Christ which leads to eternal life.* (Jude 21)

At times we may be concerned about God's mercy, even fearful that we may not be forgiven. In his epistle, Jude advises us to "persevere in God's love." As we do so, we will better understand that in his boundless mercy Jesus wants to forgive us even more than we could want forgiveness. Trusting in his merciful forgiveness pleases Jesus so much that he "leads us to eternal life."

28 *"Father, / all those you gave me / I would have in my company / where I am, / to see this glory of mine."* (Jn 17:24)

This prayer of Jesus reveals his great love for us. He loves us so much, he wants us with him for all eternity. Love always wants to be near the beloved. In turn, we want to be united with Jesus. That is the longing of every human heart.

Jesus prays that we will be with him in his glory. What comfort and consolation, what hope and reassurance we experience in knowing that the prayer of Jesus is always answered.

29 *"My sheep hear my voice. / I know them, / and they follow me. / I give them eternal life, / and they shall never perish."*

(Jn 10:27-28)

Sheep usually trust their shepherd totally. They are confident that he will lead them to verdant pastures. The image of Jesus as the Good Shepherd and us as his sheep is reassuring and comforting. If our hearts are in tune with his, we will recognize his voice. With confidence and trust, we will follow his word, which maps out a way of life for us. This pattern of life will guarantee that we will never perish, but will enjoy eternal life with the Good Shepherd in verdant pastures.

30 *"I am indeed going to prepare a place for you, / and then I shall come back to take you with me, / that where I am you also may be."*

(Jn 14:3)

Jesus knows that the road through life can be rough and rocky. He knows that there will be moments of doubt and discouragement, of fear and fatigue, of hesitation and hardship. He illumines our way with the reassuring beam of hope that he is personally accompanying us and taking us with him. He will not relinquish his loving care until we are securely in the community of perfect love in the Holy Trinity.

31 *Eye has not seen, ear has not heard, / nor has it so much as dawned on man / what God has prepared for those who love him.*

(1 Cor 2:9)

Prophets and seers, poets and preachers have futilely tried to give us a verbal delineation of the glory and grandeur of heaven. Paul, recalling Isaiah, tells us that we cannot even conjure up in our imagination "what God has prepared for those who love him." All we can say is that all of us want to be loved, and in heaven we will experience infinite love.

Only goodness and kindness follow me
   all the days of my life;
And I shall dwell in the house of the Lord
   for years to come. (Ps 23:6)